the yarn girls' guide
to beyond the basics

the yarn girls' guide
to beyond the basics

JULIE CARLES AND JORDANA JACOBS

PHOTOGRAPHS BY ELLEN SILVERMAN

ILLUSTRATIONS BY DANIELLA COHN AND GAIL CADDEN

POTTER CRAFT

NEW YORK

Copyright © 2005
by Julie Carles and
Jordana Jacobs
Photographs copyright © 2005
by Ellen Silverman

Published in the United States
by Potter Craft, an imprint of the
Crown Publishing Group, a division of
Random House, Inc., New York.
www.crownpublishing.com
www.clarksonpotter.com

POTTER CRAFT and CLARKSON N. POTTER
are trademarks and POTTER
and colophon are registered trademarks of
Random House, Inc.

Portions of this work previously appeared in
The Yarn Girls' Guide to Simple Knits
(Clarkson Potter, 2002) and *The Yarn Girls' Guide*
to Kid Knits (Clarkson Potter, 2004).

Library of Congress Cataloging-in-Publication Data
Carles, Julie.
The yarn girls' guide to beyond the basics /
Julie Carles and Jordana Jacobs.— 1st ed.
1. Knitting—Patterns.   2. Knitwear.
I. Jacobs, Jordana.   II. Title.
TT825.C1797   2005
746.43'20432—dc22   2004028752

ISBN 1-4000-9798-3

Printed in China

Design by Jennifer K. Beal

1   3   5   7   9   10   8   6   4   2

First Edition

dedication

To our families: Jeff, John, Max, and Olivia.

acknowledgments

We want to thank everybody involved in making this book. Rosy Ngo, our great editor, who also moonlights as a model. Jenny Beal, who worked so hard on the design of the book and made it look as beautiful as she is. Ellen Silverman, for the wonderful photographs, and her assistant, Christina, who is a gorgeous model as well as a talented computer whiz. Elise, who made everyone more beautiful than they thought they could be. Suzanne Pincus, our irreplaceable manager, who does it all—models, edits, writes, and keeps us sane. Petra Marcel, the real boss. Mercedes Bravo, whose fingers fly as she knits our samples. Leslie, for helping us out with some last-minute knitting. And the rest of the people who work so hard at The Yarn Company: Nici, Rachel, Jennifer, Laura, Helen, Josh, Cara, Maureen, Leslie, and Lisa. Our other fabulous models: Julien Yoo, Tara Baghwan, Mindy Miller, and Karen Abbe. Our agent, Carla Glasser, who can always iron out the rough spots diplomatically. And Daniella Tineo Cohn and Gail Cadden, for the crisp and clear illustrations that have taught so many people how to knit.

Finally, we would like to thank all our customers and everybody out there who has helped to make the Yarn Girls a reality.

contents

introduction

Knitting is taking America by storm.
But despite this knit mania, it is still difficult to find a book
of patterns that are stylish, quick to knit, and simple.

The objective of our first book, *The Yarn Girls' Guide to
Simple Knits,* was to provide such patterns. It contains thirty
easy-to-knit patterns for popular sweater shapes, ponchos,
hats, scarves, and blankets. The projects are all knit on large
needles (size US 9 or larger), which knit up quickly to give
knitters a sense of accomplishment in only a short period of
time. The response to this book was excellent. People
appreciate the simple styles and the ease with which they
are able to complete the projects.

Our second book, *The Yarn Girls' Guide to Kid Knits,*
follows the same premise as the first book—simple styles,
quick knits, and a wearable end product—with a few
changes. The difference is twofold: First, our focus was on
offering stylish knits for babies and toddlers. Second, the
chapters are broken down into two categories, "basics" and
"beyond basics." The basic projects are similar to those in
The Yarn Girls' Guide to Simple Knits in that they are knit in
garter stitch or stockinette stitch. The "beyond basics," however, add a little something extra to the fundamental
shapes, be it a little color or a different stitch. These "beyond
basic" garments are still simple but they allow the knitter to
advance in his or her skills, upping the "wow" factor.

We came up with the idea for this book when writing
Kid Knits. A whole book of "beyond basics" for adults
seemed like the perfect next book. We thought that everybody who enjoyed our first book is probably ready for a new
challenge in their knitting. And we thought that those who
passed on the first book because it was just too simple may
appreciate this one.

The Yarn Girls' Guide to Beyond the Basics is a great
opportunity for beginners who have mastered the basic knit
and purl stitches to learn some new, but still simple, techniques. Each chapter here contains one "basic" sweater at
the beginning. Then there are two or three other projects
that each contain a new challenge. Some projects are
shaped slightly differently than our basic sweaters; there
are A-lines and raglans. Some projects use color techniques
such as basic stripes, single-row stripes, and intarsia. And
some incorporate new stitches such as slip stitches, yarn
overs, and cables. Whichever hurdle you choose to jump, be
assured that the directions are written clearly and the step-
by-step instructions (found in the appendix) will help you
through the rough patches. Also, we include illustrations for
all the techniques used as well as many new definitions and
explanations of terms you may not have encountered
previously. We hope you enjoy knitting these patterns as
much as we loved developing them.

the yarn girls' guide
to the fundamentals
and more

If it's been a while since you've picked up your knitting needles or if you're just feeling a little rusty on the fundamentals, this section includes a quick review of basic knitting techniques. You can turn here for directions on knitting, purling, casting on, making a slip knot, ribbing, increasing, decreasing, and yarn overs. This section also includes detailed instructions for the more advanced methods used throughout this book. If you've never knit a cable before and want to give it a try, just look at the diagrams on page 27. Or if you're knitting One Singular Sensation (page 84) and wondering how to make those single-row stripes, just look here. Also included in this section are how-to techniques to help you finish your sweater. You will learn how to sew your seams together and pick up stitches for neck and button bands. We have also included instructions for finishing touches, such as basic crochet stitches, fringe, I-cords, and tassels.

THE VERY BASICS
slip knot and cast on

Even before you begin to knit, you must cast the necessary number of stitches onto your needle.

To do this, you have to measure out a length of yarn for a "tail," which will become your cast-on stitches. The length of the tail determines how many stitches you can cast on; the more stitches you are casting on, the longer the tail must be. Our rule of thumb is that an arm's length—that is, the distance from your wrist to your shoulder—of yarn will yield 20 stitches on the needle.

After you measure out the tail, make a slip knot, which will also be your first cast-on stitch. Place this on a needle, hold that needle in your right hand, and continue to cast on stitches until you have the required number on the needle.

to make a slip knot

1. Measure out the required length of yarn and, with the free end hanging, make a loop at the measured point. You should see an *X*. (Illus. A)

2. Grab hold of the strand of yarn that is on the top of the *X* and bring this strand behind and through the loop. (Illus. B)

3. Hold this new loop in one hand and pull on the loose ends to create your slip knot! (Illus. C & D)

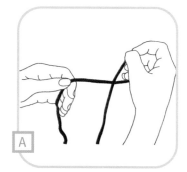
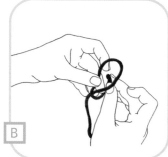

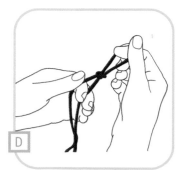

to cast on

1. Place your slip knot on a needle. Hold the needle in your right hand pointing toward the left. Hold the slip knot in place with your right index finger so it does not fly off the needle. (Illus. A)

2. Place the thumb and index finger of your left hand between the 2 strands of yarn dangling from the needle. (Your thumb should be closer to you and the index finger away from you.) Hold the dangling yarn taut with your ring and pinky fingers. (Illus. B)

3. Flip your left thumb up while guiding the needle down and to the left. A loop should form around your thumb. (Illus. C)

4. Guide the needle up through the loop on your thumb. (Illus. D)

5. Guide the needle over the yarn that is around your index finger and catch it with the needle. (Illus. E)

6. Guide the yarn hooked by the needle down through the loop around your thumb. (Illus. F) Slip your thumb out of its loop and place this thumb inside the strand of yarn that is closer to you. Pull down gently. Now you have a cast-on stitch!

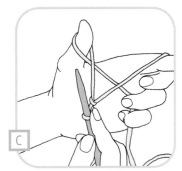

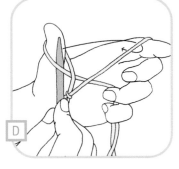

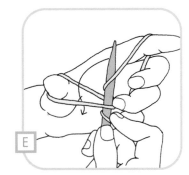

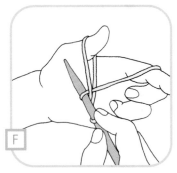

knit and purl

to knit

1. Cast on the desired number of stitches. Hold the needle with the cast-on stitches in your left hand and the empty needle in your right hand. Point the needles toward each other. (Illus. A)

2. While holding the yarn in the back, insert the right needle from front to back through the first stitch on the left needle. You will see that the needles form an *X* with the right needle beneath the left needle. (Illus. B)

3. Keep the needles crossed by holding both needles with the thumb, index, and middle fingers of your left hand. With your right hand, pick up the yarn and wrap it under and around the bottom needle; do not wrap it around the left needle. (Illus. C)

4. Hold the yarn in place around the right needle between your right thumb and index finger and guide the right needle toward you through the center of the stitch on the left needle. (Illus. D) The right needle should now be on top of the left needle. (Illus. E)

5. Pull the remaining yarn off the left needle by pulling the right needle up and to the right so the newly formed stitch slides off the left needle to the right. You will have a newly created stitch on the right needle. (Illus. F)

6. Repeat steps 1 through 5 across the entire row of stitches.

NOTE:

WHEN YOU FINISH KNITTING THE ENTIRE ROW, ALL OF YOUR STITCHES WILL BE ON THE RIGHT NEEDLE. NOW PLACE THE EMPTY NEEDLE IN YOUR RIGHT HAND AND THE NEEDLE WITH THE STITCHES ON IT IN YOUR LEFT HAND. NOW YOU ARE READY TO BEGIN KNITTING ANOTHER ROW.

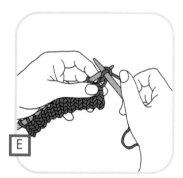

to purl

1. Hold the needle with the stitches in your left hand and the empty needle in your right hand and the loose yarn hanging in front of your work. The needles should be pointed toward each other. (Illus. A)

2. Insert the right needle back to front through the front of the first stitch on the left needle. The needles will form an X with the right needle on top of the left needle. Make sure the yarn is in front of the needle. (Illus. B)

3. Keep the needles crossed in the X position by holding both needles with the thumb, index, and middle fingers of your left hand. Wrap the yarn over and around the front needle from the back, bringing the yarn around and in front of the right needle. (Illus. C)

4. Holding the yarn in place around the needle with the thumb and index finger of your right hand, push the right needle down and toward the back through the center of the stitch on the left needle. (Illus. D) The right needle will now be behind the left needle. (Illus. E)

5. Pull the remaining yarn off the left needle by pulling the right needle to the right so the newly formed stitch slides off the left needle onto the right needle. (Illus. F)

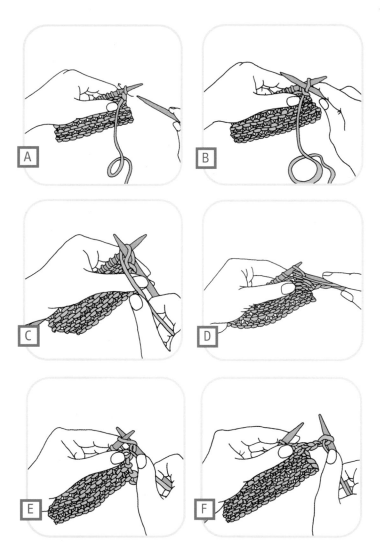

stockinette stitch

Now you know how to knit and purl. If you alternate knitting a row and purling a row, you will be working in the most commonly used stitch, the stockinette stitch. This is universally abbreviated as **St st.** If you just knit or just purl on every row, then you are working in the garter stitch.

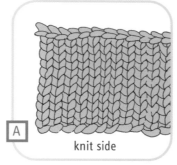

A — knit side

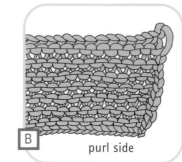

B — purl side

ribbing

The illustrations here show a Knit 2, Purl 2 ribbing.

to make a ribbing

1. Knit 2 stitches. (Illus. A)

2. Separate the needles slightly and bring the yarn from the back of your work to the front. Be sure you bring the yarn between the needles and not over a needle (which would cause you to add a stitch). (Illus. B)

3. Purl 2 stitches. (Illus. C)

4. After purling, you must bring the yarn between the needles to the back of the work before you knit the next 2 stitches. (Illus. D)

5. Repeat these steps for your ribbing. Note how knit stitches (*V*s) are over knit stitches and purl stitches are over purl stitches. (Illus. E)

A

B

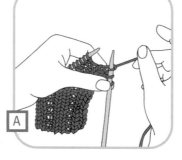

C

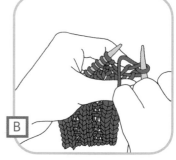

D

E

increase and decrease

INCREASING

Increasing is how you will add stitches on a needle in order to add width to your knitted piece.

You will encounter two methods for increasing in this book. The first is the bar method, known as Make 1, or **M1,** which is our preferred way to increase while knitting sleeves. Generally, we recommend you start a bar increase 2 stitches in from the edge of your work. This means you should knit 2 stitches, then do a bar increase, then knit until there are 2 stitches remaining on the left needle, then increase again. Increasing 2 stitches in from your edge makes sewing up seams much easier because you can sew down a straight line that is uninterrupted by increases.

The second kind of increase is known as knitting into the front and back of a stitch. It is a quick and easy way to increase and is generally a good choice when you want your increases at the very edge of the knitted piece. We used this method for So Many Ponchos, So Little Time (page 116).

bar method
(also referred to as make 1, or m1)

1. At the point you wish to add a stitch, pull the needles slightly apart to reveal the bar located between 2 stitches. (See arrow, Illus. A)

2. With your left needle, pick up the bar from behind. (Illus. B)

3. Knit the loop you have made. Be sure to knit this loop as you would normally knit a stitch, going from the front of the stitch to the back. (Illus. C) Sometimes this stitch is a little tight and will be difficult to knit. In that case, gently push the loop up with your left forefinger, loosening the stitch and making it easier to insert your right needle.

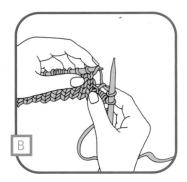

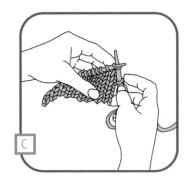

knitting into the front and back of a stitch

1. Begin to knit into the stitch you are going to increase into. Stop when you have brought the right needle through the stitch on the left needle and it is forming the *X* in the front. (Illus. A) DO NOT take the stitch off the left needle as you normally would when completing a knit stitch.

2. Leave the stitch on the left needle and move the tip of the right needle so it is behind the left needle. (Illus. B)

3. Insert the right needle into the back of the stitch on the left needle (Illus. C) and knit it again—wrap yarn under and around the back needle. Hold the yarn against the needle with your right hand and guide the needle toward you through the center of the stitch. The right needle should end up on top of the left needle.

4. Pull the stitch off the left needle. You now have 2 new stitches on the right needle. (Illus. D)

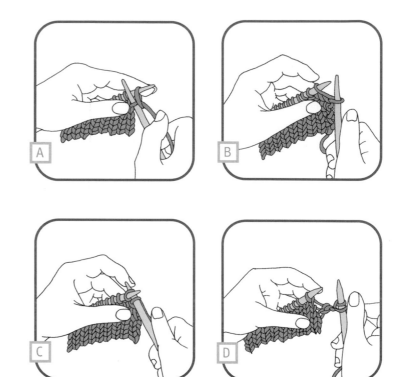

DECREASING

Decreasing is how you will reduce the number of stitches on a needle in order to narrow the width of your knitted piece.

In this book, we use two methods of decreasing. The first is a slip, slip, knit, abbreviated as **SSK.** This is a left-slanting decrease. The other method is a Knit 2 together, abbreviated as **K2tog.** This is a right-slanting decrease.

slip, slip, knit (ssk)

We use this method when we want our decreases to slant toward the *left*.

1. One at a time, slip 2 stitches as though you were going to knit them (knitwise), to the right needle. (Slipping a stitch means that you insert your right needle into the loop on the left needle as though you were going to knit it BUT you don't complete the knit stitch; you just slide the stitch off the left needle onto the right needle.) (Illus. A)

2. Insert the left needle into the front of the 2 slipped stitches, forming an *X*, with the left needle in front of the right needle. (Illus. B)

3. Wrap the yarn under and around the back needle and knit the 2 slipped stitches together, slipping the completed new stitch onto the right needle. (Illus. C & D)

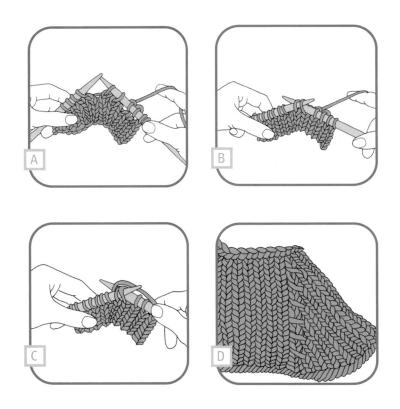

knit 2 together (k2tog)

We use this technique when we want our decreases to slant to the *right*.

1. Working on a knit row, insert your right needle from front to back into the second and then the first stitch you want to knit together. (Illus. A)

2. Bring the yarn around the needle to complete the stitch as with a regular knit stitch. (Illus. B & C)

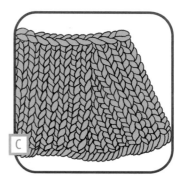

double decrease

This decrease reduces two stitches each time you do it. We use this technique in Hip and Hooded on page 110.

1. Insert the right needle into the next 2 stitches on the left needle, as if you were knitting them. (Illus. A)

2. Slip these 2 stitches to the right needle without working them. (Illus. B)

3. Knit the next stitch. (Illus. C)

4. With the left needle, pull both the slipped stitches over the knit stitch and off the needle. (Illus. D)

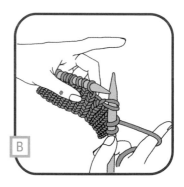

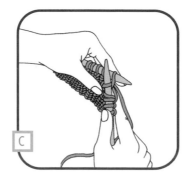

bind off

Binding off is how you get your knitted piece off the needles and prevent it from unraveling.

1. Knit 2 stitches. (Illus. A)

2. Insert the left needle into the front of the first stitch on the right needle. Using the left needle, pull the first stitch up and over the second stitch. (Illus. B) Place your forefinger on the second stitch to hold it in place and keep it from coming off the needle.

3. Now push that stitch off the left needle completely. (Illus. C & D)

4. Knit one more stitch and repeat the last two steps. Continue this process until you have bound off the desired number of stitches.

   When you have finished binding off all your stitches at the end of your work, you should have 1 loop left on the right needle. At this point, cut the yarn, leaving 3 or 4 inches, and pull the end through the remaining loop to tie it off.

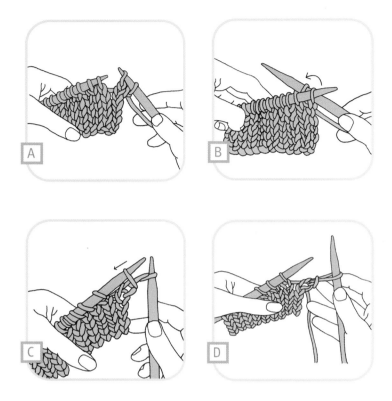

BEYOND BASIC TECHNIQUES
yarn overs

A yarn over (abbreviated **YO**) allows you to make a hole in your knitting on purpose—as opposed to those inadvertent holes made by dropping stitches. Yarn overs are generally used for lace knitting or to make a buttonhole.

yarn over before a knit

If the stitch after the yarn over will be a knit, use this method:

1. Hold both needles with the fingers of your left hand and hold the yarn with your right hand in back of the right needle. (Illus. A)

2. Pull the yarn up and around the right needle from the back to the front to the back again. (Illus. B) You have created the yarn over, which is just a loop.

yarn over before a purl

If the stitch after the yarn over will be a purl, use this method:

1. Hold both needles with the fingers of your left hand and hold the yarn with your right hand in front of the right needle. (Illus. A)

2. Pull the yarn up and around the needle, from the front to the back and to the front again. (Illus. B)

wrap yarn around needle twice

Wrapping the yarn around the needle twice is a technique that, together with dropping the extra wrap stitch on the next row, creates an elongated stitch. The double wrap is an easy way to add a little pizzazz to anything you may knit.

1. Begin to knit the stitch, wrapping the yarn under and around the bottom of the right needle. (Illus. A)

2. Wrap the yarn around the bottom of the needle one more time. (Illus. B)

3. Pull the right needle through the loop on the left needle, completing the knit stitch. (Illus. C & D)

4. When you work the next row, whether you are knitting or purling, insert the needle into only 1 loop (the first wrap) and drop the extra loop off the left needle to allow the stitch to lengthen.

5. This is what your elongated stitch will look like. (Illus. E)

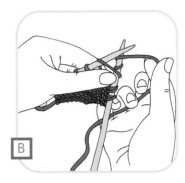

A

B

C

D

NOTE:
TO MAKE EVEN LONGER STITCHES YOU CAN WRAP THE YARN AROUND THE NEEDLE 3 OR 4 TIMES.

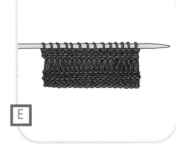

E

slip stitch

Slipped stitches add interest and texture to a knitted fabric. Although it may sound tricky, making a slip stitch is easier than knitting and purling.

1. Insert the right needle into the stitch on the left needle as if to purl.

2. Move this stitch to the right needle. The yarn will be attached to the stitch preceding the slipped stitch.

A

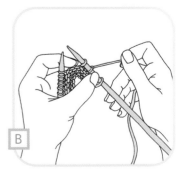

B

color work

We use two types of color work in our patterns. Striping is the easiest way to incorporate different colored yarns into a knitted project. Once your colors are attached (just as simple as starting a new ball of yarn), all you need to do is drop the color you are working with and pick up the color you need to use next. You begin and end a stripe at the beginning of a row. Intarsia is a technique used to add or change color in the middle of a row. For this book, we used only two colors at a time so you don't need to use bobbins (holders for a small amount of yarn); you can use the whole balls of yarn.

multirow striping

1. Work the number of desired rows in color A. Leave the yarn of color A attached. (Illus. A)

2. Add in color B by looping the new yarn around the right needle (Illus. B) and knitting the first stitch.

3. Work the number of desired rows in color B.

4. To switch to color A, let go of color B and pick up color A. (Illus. C & D)

5. Knit with color A for the number of desired rows. (Illus. E)

6. Continue striping until the required length. (Illus. F)

   If you are making very wide stripes, you might prefer to cut the yarn each time you switch colors. Otherwise, just leave the unused yarn hanging until it is time to alternate colors.

HELPFUL HINT:
WHEN WORKING IN A STRIPE PATTERN, COUNT THE NUMBER OF STRIPES TO MAKE SURE YOU HAVE KNIT THE SAME NUMBER OF ROWS UP TO THE ARMHOLE AND TO THE TOP OF THE SWEATER.

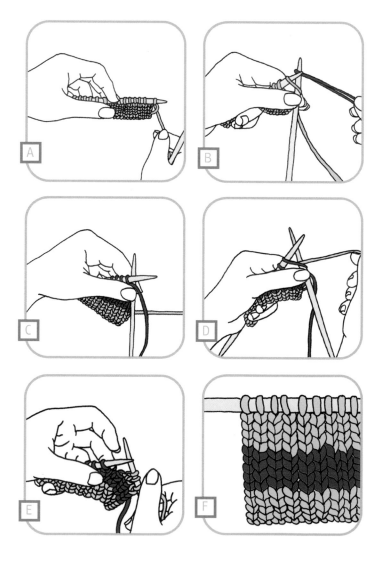

single-row striping

Unlike the usual technique for making wider stripes, you need to work each color over an odd number of rows. This means that your yarn will never be in the correct place to use again unless you cut it and then tie it on at the other end where you need it. Doing that, however, leaves lots of unwanted ends, which will need to be woven in. Our method for single-row striping allows knitters to carry the yarn up their work as they would with even-row striping. This method actually works with any striping that involves an odd number of rows.

NOTE:

YOU CANNOT USE STRAIGHT NEE-DLES WHEN EMPLOYING THIS TECHNIQUE; YOU MUST USE CIR-CULAR NEEDLES.

1. Knit with color A. (Illus. A)

2. Slide stitches to the right end of the needle. (Illus. B)

3. Knit with color B. (Illus. C)

4. You are now ready to purl. Color A and color B are now at the same end of the needle. (Illus. D)

5. Purl with color A. (Illus. E)

6. Color A and color B are now at different ends of the needle. Slide stitches to the right end of the needle where color B is. (Illus. F)

7. Purl with color B. (Illus. G)

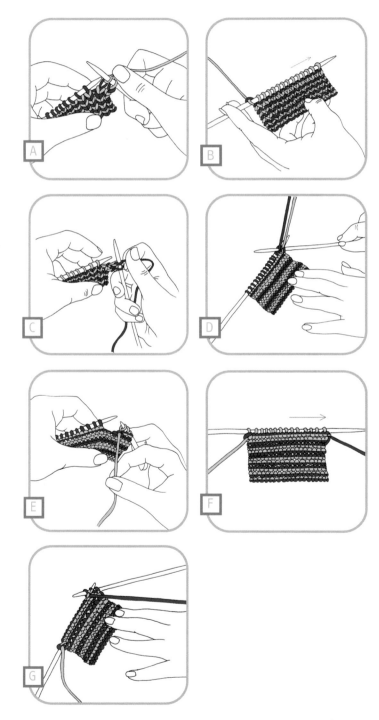

intarsia

1. Cast on the desired number of stitches with color A and color B. (Illus. A)

2. Knit across the stitches of color B, then pick up color A and bring it under color B. (Illus. B)

3. Begin knitting the stitches in color A. (Illus. C)

4. Purl across the stitches of color A. (Illus. D)

5. Pick up color B and bring it under color A and then begin purling the stitches in color B. (Illus. E)

6. This is what the knit side of your work should look like. (Illus. F)

7. This is what the purl side of your work should look like. (Illus. G)

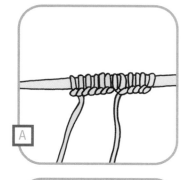

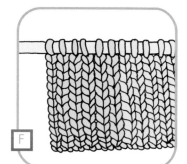

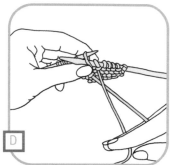

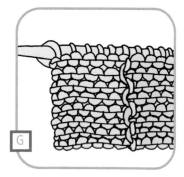

cables

Basically, cables are made by twisting the order of the stitches. Simple or complicated, cables are all based on the same premise: rearranging the stitches on the needle so they cross over to create a twist. To rearrange the order of stitches, you need a cable needle. There are various types of cable needles but they all have the same function. There are J-hooks, metal ones with a bump in the center, and wooden ones that are straight—we personally like the straight wooden ones because wood is generally less slippery than metal and holds the stitches on the cable needle better.

A basic cable stitch pattern reads like this: C8B or C12F. The C stands for cable. The number in the middle denotes the total number of stitches that the cable is worked over. You will divide this number in half to determine how many stitches to put on the cable needle. The B or F stands for back or front and indicates where you will hold the stitches on the cable needle while you are knitting the stitches from the left needle. We tend to like back cables because they can be done without cable needles if you are in a pinch—just pass over the group of stitches that would normally go on the cable needle and knit the required number of stitches from the left needle. Then take the right needle and twist it a little and knit the first stitches. Pull all the stitches off the left needle together.

1. Slip required number of stitches onto a cable needle, purlwise. Hold these stitches at the back (or front) of the work, as indicated in the pattern. (Illus. A)

2. Knit the required number of stitches off the left needle. (Illus. B)

3. Knit the stitches off the cable needle. (Illus. C)

4. This is what a finished cable will look like. (Illus. D)

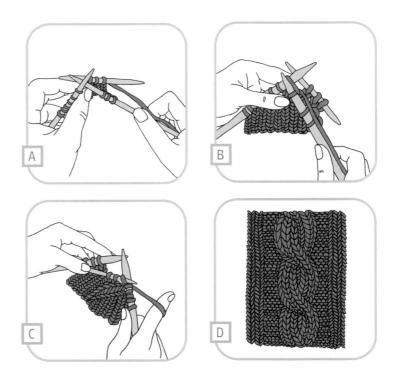

cast on at the end of the row

You are going to need to use this technique when knitting Toasty Ears (page 123). When beginning this project, you will cast on stitches as you normally would for half of the back. Next, knit across the stitches of the first ear flap. Then use this technique to cast on stitches for the front of the hat.

1. Insert the right needle into the first stitch on the left needle and knit it, but do not take the new stitch off the left needle. (Illus. A)

2. Bring the left needle to the front and right of the stitch on the right needle and then insert the left needle into the stitch on the right needle. (Illus. B)

3. Transfer the stitch from the right to the left needle. (Illus. C)

   You have now cast on 1 stitch. Repeat these steps until you have cast on the desired number of stitches.

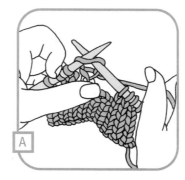

FINISHING TECHNIQUES

You can spend hours knitting row after row of perfect ribbing and flawless stockinette stitch, but all those efforts can be undermined by sloppy finishing technique. Knowing how to sew a sweater together properly is the ultimate key to whether the sweater looks handmade—or homemade. If you use the proper techniques, the process should be relatively painless and your sweater should look virtually seamless. And a final steaming, known as blocking, will smooth over any inconsistencies or bumpy seams.

Some tips:

* Sweaters are always sewn on the right side.

* Although other people might tell you differently, we prefer **not** to use the yarn we knit our sweater with to sew it together. Generally, we suggest using a needlepoint yarn in a similar color because using a different yarn allows you to see what you are doing much more clearly. And, dare we say it, it also enables you to rip out what you have done, if necessary, without inadvertently damaging the sweater itself.

Whether you are making a V-neck, a turtleneck, a crewneck, or a cardigan, sweaters are always assembled in the same order:

1. Sew shoulder seams together.

2. Sew sleeves onto sweater.

3. Sew sleeve seams from armhole to cuff.

4. Sew side seams from armhole to waist.

Once the pieces are joined together, you can add crochet edgings, pick up stitches for a neck, create button bands for a cardigan, or embellish with other finishing touches.

sewing shoulder seams

1. Lay the front and back of your sweater flat with the right sides facing you and the shoulders pointing toward each other. If you are sewing the shoulder seams of a cardigan together, make sure the armholes are facing away from the center and the neck toward the center. (Illus. A)

2. Cut a piece of sewing yarn approximately twice the width of your shoulder seam and thread it through a darning needle.

3. Secure the sewing yarn to the garment by making a knot with one end of the sewing yarn on the inside shoulder edge of the back of your sweater.

4. Insert the needle into the first stitch at the shoulder edge of the front of the sweater. Your needle should have passed under 2 bars and should be on the right side or outside of the work. (Illus. B)

5. Now place the needle under the corresponding stitch of the back of your sweater. (Illus. C) Next your needle will go into the hole that the yarn is coming from on the front and you will go under the next stitch. You will do the same thing on the back now. This is how you continue to weave the sweater together. It is easier if you keep the yarn relatively loose because

it is easier to see the hole that your yarn is coming from. Pull the sewing yarn tight after you have 6 or 7 stitches and just loosen the last stitch before you proceed.

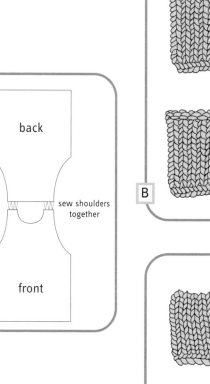

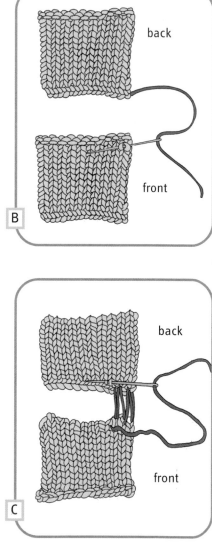

sewing the sleeves to the body

A

B

C

D

This is possibly the most difficult aspect of finishing your sweater because it is really the only part where something must fit into something else. The cap of your sleeve must fit *perfectly* into your armhole. (Illus. A) That said, sometimes it is possible to fudge it a little to make it work.

1. Cut a piece of yarn approximately 30 inches and thread it through a darning needle.

2. Attach the yarn to the body of the sweater by poking the needle through the edge of the shoulder seam that you made when sewing the shoulders together. Pull the yarn halfway through and make a knot. You should now have half the yarn going down one side of the armhole and half going down the other side.

3. Find the center of the upper sleeve edge by folding the sleeve in half. With the darning needle, pull the yarn under the center 2 bars on the sleeve. (Illus. B) Your sleeve is now attached to the body of the sweater.

4. Now you need to find 2 bars on the body of the sweater. Start at the top near the shoulder seam. This is slightly different from finding the bars on the sleeves because the bars on the sleeves are stitches and on the body, the bars will be rows. Place the needle 1 full stitch in on the body of the sweater and find the 2 bars.

5. Continue sewing as for the shoulders, taking 2 bars from the body and 2 bars from the sleeve and pulling the yarn every few stitches until the sewing yarn is no longer visible and until the sleeve is sewn into the armhole. (Illus. C & D)

sewing side and sleeve seams

1. Cut a piece of yarn approximately twice the length of the sleeve and side seam.

2. Attach the yarn by inserting the sewing needle through the 2 seams at the underarm. Pull the yarn halfway through and make a knot. Half of the yarn should be used to sew the side seam and half should be used to sew the sleeve seam.

3. It doesn't matter whether you start with the body or the sleeve. For both, find the 2 vertical bars 1 full stitch in from the edge and begin the sewing process (Illus. A), taking 2 bars from one side of the sweater and then 2 bars from the other side. (Illus. B) Make sure you are going into the hole where the yarn last came out and pulling the yarn every few stitches. (Illus. C)

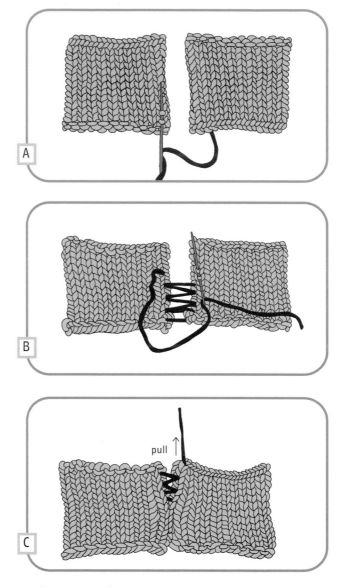

sewing up rolled edges

When sewing up a project that has rolled edges, you will want to finish it so you don't see the seam when the fabric rolls. Start by sewing your seam as you always do, on the right side of the work, BUT at about 1 inch or so before you reach the bottom, you must start sewing on the wrong side of the work instead of the right side. The seam will then show up on the right side, but the rolled edge will cover it.

sewing a raglan sweater together

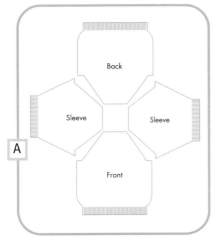

Back

Sleeve

Sleeve

A

Front

Raglan sweaters look intimidating to sew together but they are actually easier than a set-in sleeve because the sleeve seams always fit perfectly since you have knit the same number of rows for all the raglan pieces. The easiest way to begin sewing a raglan sweater together is to place all the pieces flat on a smooth surface so the front and back are opposite each other and the sleeves fit into the armholes on opposite sides. (Illus. A) You will sew all the raglan pieces together first. Start at the armhole and sew up to the neck. You will be sewing a sleeve piece to a body piece each time—there will be 4 seams in total here. Once this is done, fold the sweater in half and sew up the side and sleeve seams as you would on a set-in or drop-sleeve sweater.

weaving in ends

While you are knitting, try to keep your ends about 4 inches long. Remember this when you are adding a new ball of yarn or casting on or binding off. If the ends are long enough, you can weave them in with a sewing needle. All you do is thread the needle with an end and weave the yarn back and forth through the seam 3 to 4 times. Then snip the end. You do not need to make a knot. If the ends are too short, you can use a crochet hook.

blocking

Sometimes when a garment is completely assembled, it requires a bit of shaping. Blocking allows you to reshape the piece gently by applying steam, which relaxes the yarn fibers so they can be stretched in order to smooth out bulky seams, even out uneven knitting, or even enlarge a too-small garment.

Not every piece needs to be blocked; use your common sense. But if you decide reshaping or smoothing is in order, pin your garment onto a padded ironing board, easing it into the desired shape. If your iron can emit a strong stream of steam, hold the iron above the piece without touching it and saturate it with steam. Otherwise, dampen a towel, place it over the garment, and press with a warm iron. Allow the piece to remain pinned to the ironing board until it is completely cool.

Never apply a hot iron directly to a knitted piece, and always read the label on your yarn before blocking; some fibers should not be blocked.

picking up stitches

Once the pieces of your sweater are joined, you need to make nice finished edges and button bands. Rather than knit these elements as separate pieces that are then sewn on, we like to knit them directly onto the finished sweater. In order to do this, you must pick up stitches along the finished edges. When you pick up the stitches for a neck, you are generally picking up stitches horizontally in an already-made stitch. When picking up for button bands, you pick up the stitches vertically, in rows. Either way, the method for picking up the stitches is the same; the difference is where you place the needle to pick up the next stitch. You can pick up stitches in existing stitches (vertically, Illus. A–E) or in rows (horizontally, Illus. F–J).

1. Place the work with the right side facing you. Starting at the right edge of your piece with the knitting needle in your right hand, place the needle in the first stitch, poking through from the outside to the inside. (Illus. A & B; F & G)

2. Loop the yarn under and around the needle and pull the needle back through that same stitch. There should be 1 stitch on the needle. (Illus. C & D; H & I)

3. Continue to poke the needle through each stitch, wrapping the yarn around the needle as if you were knitting and adding a stitch to the needle each time. (Illus. E & J)

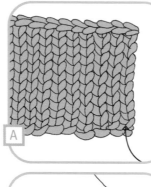

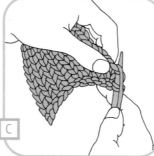

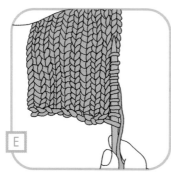

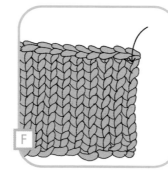

helpful hint

When you are picking up stitches in stitches, as for a crewneck pullover, most of the time you want to pick up every stitch. It is important to note that there is an extra hole between each stitch. So picking up every stitch is the same thing as picking up every other hole. If you poke your needle through every consecutive hole, you will pick up too many stitches.

When you are picking up stitches in rows, as when you are picking up button bands, you do not want to pick up a stitch in *every* row. To determine how often to pick up, note your gauge. If your gauge is 3 stitches to the inch, then you will want to pick up stitches in 3 consecutive rows, then skip 1 row and repeat this process. If your gauge is 4 stitches to the inch, you will want to pick up stitches in 4 consecutive rows and then skip 1 row. It is necessary to skip a row every so often because there are more rows per inch than stitches per inch. If you were to pick up a stitch in every row, when you started to knit these picked-up stitches, you would have too many stitches and the button bands would look wavy.

FINISHING TOUCHES

Fringe, I-cords, and tassels are nice accents on hats, scarves, blankets, and ponchos. Before you begin, you will need a few things. For fringe, you will need a piece of cardboard, a crochet hook, a pair of scissors, and yarn. For an I-cord, you need a circular or double-pointed needle and yarn. For tassels, you need a piece of cardboard, scissors, and yarn.

fringe

To make the fringe, cut a piece of cardboard as tall as the length of fringe you desire. Then wrap the yarn around the cardboard approximately 20 times. (If you need more fringe than this, you can repeat the step.) Cut the strands of yarn across the top of the cardboard. You now have strands of yarn that are twice your desired length. If you want thick fringe, use several strands of yarn; if you want thinner fringe, use only a strand or two.

VERY IMPORTANT:

TO FILL IN THE FRINGE ON A PIECE OF WORK, WE SUGGEST YOU START BY ATTACHING FRINGE AT EACH EDGE AND THEN AT EACH MIDWAY POINT UNTIL YOU ARE SATISFIED.

1. To attach fringe to your knitted garment, insert your crochet hook through a stitch at one of the ends of your knitted piece. You should take the crochet hook from underneath the piece to the top of it, and the crochet hook should be facing you. (Illus. A)

2. Fold your strands of yarn in half and grab the center of these strands with your hook. Pull these strands through the stitch. (Illus. B & C)

3. Remove the crochet hook and place your fingers through the loop you made with the strands of yarn. Then pull the loose ends through this loop. (Illus. D & E)

4. You have completed one fringe. (Illus. F) Even up the ends by trimming them.

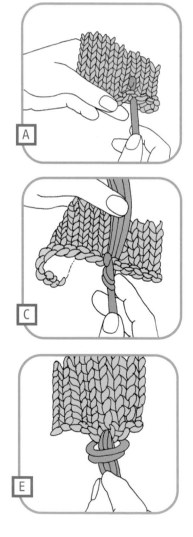

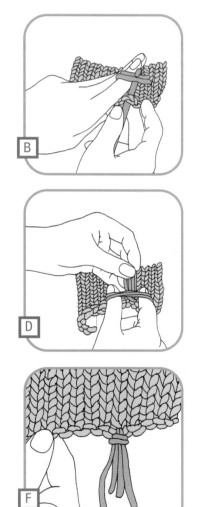

i-cords

You can add I-cords, which are basically knitted ropes, to the top of a hat to add a little pizzazz. They can be used as purse handles and as cords in a hooded sweatshirt.

1. Using a double-pointed or circular needle, cast on and knit 3 stitches. (Illus. A)

2. Slide these stitches toward the right to the other end of the needle. (Illus. B)

3. Place the needle in your left hand. The yarn will be attached to the stitch farthest to the left. (Illus. C)

4. Pick the yarn up from behind and knit the 3 stitches. (Illus. D & E)

5. Repeat steps 2–4 until your I-cord reaches the desired length.

6. This is what your I-cord should look like. (Illus. F)

7. To end the I-cord, K3tog, cut the yarn, and pull the tail through the remaining loop to fasten.

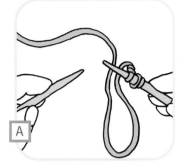

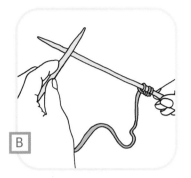

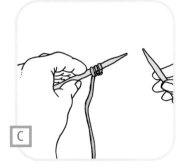

tassels

Tassels are another fun option when adding details to hats. They also look great on a blanket or a poncho.

1. Cut a piece of cardboard a little longer than you want your tassel to be. Wind yarn around the cardboard tightly to desired thickness. (Illus. A)

2. Slide a strand of yarn between the yarn and the cardboard so each loose strand of yarn is on either side. (Illus. B)

3. Tie the strand closed. (Illus. C)

4. Cut the strands of yarn on the bottom end of the cardboard (Illus. D) and remove the cardboard.

5. Tie a strand of yarn around the bundle about 1 inch from the top of the tassel. (Illus. E)

6. Pull this yarn through the center of the top of the tassel and attach to your knitted garment. (Illus. F)

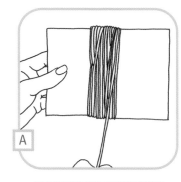

A

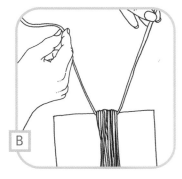

B

C

D

E

F

single crochet
and shrimp stitch

Even if you have never crocheted—and never plan to—it's useful to know a couple of basic crochet techniques for finishing off a knitted piece. Crochet edgings give sweaters and throws a nice, polished look. Shrimp stitch gives a sturdy corded look. Generally, you want to use a crochet hook that matches the size of the knitting needle you used. For instance, if you used a size 6 knitting needle, you should use a size 6 (also known as size G) crochet hook.

single crochet

1. With the right side of the work facing you, insert your crochet hook through a stitch under the bind-off. (Illus. A)

2. Grab the yarn with the crochet hook and pull it through the stitch to the front of your work. (Illus. B) You will now have 1 loop on the crochet hook. (Illus. C)

3. Insert the crochet hook through the next stitch, hook the yarn, and pull it through the stitch. You now have 2 loops on the crochet hook. (Illus. D & E)

4. Hook the yarn and pull it through both of the loops on the crochet hook. (Illus. F) You will end up with 1 loop on the hook. Insert the hook through the next stitch and repeat across the entire row, ending with 1 loop on the hook.

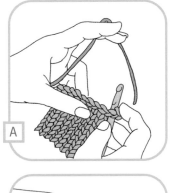
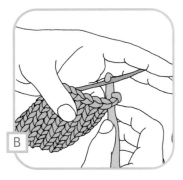
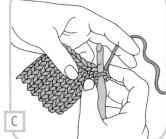

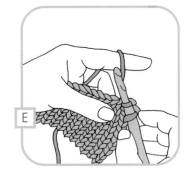

shrimp stitch

This is also known as backwards crochet because you work from left to right instead of right to left. You must do 1 row of single crochet (abbreviated **SC**) before you begin the shrimp stitch.

1. Make a slip stitch by grabbing the yarn through the loop on the hook. (Illus. A)

2. Keeping your right index finger on the loop, insert the hook into the next stitch from the right side to the wrong side of the work. (Illus. B & C)

3. Grab the yarn with the hook and pull it through to the right side of the work. (Illus. D)

4. You should have 2 loops on the hook. (Illus. E)

5. Grab the yarn with the hook and pull it through the 2 loops. (Illus. F & G)

6. Repeat in the next stitch to the right. (Illus. H)

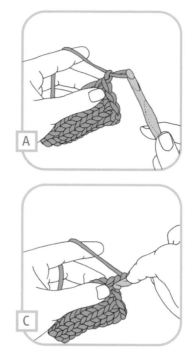

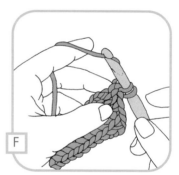

HELPFUL HINTS
make a gauge

THE MOST IMPORTANT MESSAGE IN THIS CHAPTER IS THAT
YOU MUST ALWAYS MAKE A GAUGE SWATCH!
IF YOU DON'T MAKE A GAUGE SWATCH, THERE ARE NO GUARANTEES THAT YOUR
SWEATER WILL FIT PROPERLY!

You just spent time and money picking out yarn to make the perfect sweater. You're eager to get to work and, most of all, you can't wait to see how this new addition to your wardrobe fits. In order for this scenario to have a happy ending, it is crucial that you understand gauge. A grasp of gauge will save you the misery of having to rip out your knitting because your hoped-for size small looks like it could fit an elephant. And it will help you avoid the depression that comes from investing hours of time on an unwearable garment. If you're not yet a master of gauge, read this information carefully!

STITCH GAUGE = THE NUMBER OF STITCHES REQUIRED TO PRODUCE 1 INCH OF KNITTED FABRIC

Gauge is the most important—and most misunderstood—element of knitting. Simply put, stitch gauge determines the finished measurements of your garment. Technically—and yes, it is a technical, even mathematical concept—stitch gauge tells you the number of stitches you'll need to knit to produce a piece of knitted fabric 1 inch wide.

For each pattern in this book you will find the garment's finished measurements. If your gauge is off, the finished knitted piece will not have the proper dimensions for the size you have chosen. It is, therefore, important to refer to these finished measurements as you knit, making certain your gauge has not changed and that the finished piece will have the correct measurements.

A pattern is always written with a specific gauge in mind, and if you do not get the gauge just right, your project won't turn out as the pattern designer intended.

Here's a simple example: If a pattern says your stitch gauge should be 3 stitches to the inch, that means 60 stitches should produce a piece of knitted fabric 20 inches wide. This is because 60 stitches divided by 3 (your gauge) equals 20 inches. If your gauge were 4 stitches to the inch, you would need to cast on 80 stitches to produce the same 20-inch width.

It really is just that easy: simple division and multiplication, and you can even use a calculator—we do!

All patterns state the stitch gauge (or tension, if it's not an American pattern) required to achieve the desired measurements for your finished garment. The gauge swatch is always knit in the same stitch you'll use for the garment itself. Usually a pattern will tell you that your stitch gauge should be measured over 4 inches (or 10 centimeters if, again, it's not American). For example, under "gauge" your pattern may say "16 stitches = 4 inches." This means that your stitch gauge should be 4 stitches to the inch. Patterns also generally include a row gauge, which indicates how many rows you need to knit in order to get a piece of knitted fabric 1 inch long. For most of the patterns in this book, row gauge is not particularly important, but when knitting a raglan sweater, pay close attention to the row gauge, also.

Along with the gauge, patterns also recommend a needle size to get a particular stitch gauge with a particular yarn. DO NOT assume that just because you are using a pattern's suggested yarn and needle size you don't have to do a gauge swatch. Everybody knits differently. Some people are loose knitters, some are tight knitters, and some are in the middle. Whatever type of knitter you are, you can always get the required gauge eventually, but you may need to make some adjustments. Tight knitters will have to go up in needle size, while loose knitters will have to use needles a size smaller. Remember, it's far more important to get the specified gauge than to use the specified needle–or yarn, for that matter.

Here's how to check your gauge:

- Cast on 4 times the number of stitches required per inch. For example, if the gauge is 4 stitches = 1 inch, cast on 16 stitches; if your gauge is supposed to be 3 stitches = 1 inch, cast on 12 stitches.

- Work in the pattern stitch using the needle size recommended for the body of the sweater. Sometimes ribbing is knit on smaller needles, but you shouldn't use the smaller size for your gauge.

- When your swatch is approximately 4 inches long, slip it off the needle and place it on a flat surface. Measure the width of your swatch. If it measures 4 inches wide, you're getting the required gauge and can begin your knitting project.

- If your swatch is more than 4 inches wide, your knitting is too loose. Reknit your swatch on needles a size or two smaller and measure again. Repeat as necessary, using smaller needles until you get the correct gauge.

- If your swatch is less than 4 inches wide, your knitting is too tight. Reknit your swatch on needles a size or two larger and measure the swatch again. Repeat as necessary, using larger needles until you get the correct gauge.

You should also know that gauge can change as you make your garment. This happens for a multitude of reasons and does not mean you are a bad knitter. Please check the width of what you are knitting once the piece measures about 3 inches long. Compare it to the measurements the pattern provides and make adjustments in the needle size if necessary.

REMEMBER:
Always knit a gauge
swatch–*always!!*

stuff that may help you along the way

We know you want to get to the good stuff—the patterns—but if you read over these helpful hints and keep them in mind as you knit, you might save yourself from ripping out rows of stitches or untangling a gaggle of knots.

using multiple strands of yarn

In some patterns, we used more than one strand of yarn. This means we knit with two or more strands of yarn as though they were one. We did this because we really liked a certain yarn, but it wasn't thick enough as a single strand. To use multiple strands of yarn, you can wind the separate balls into one ball. We find this easier than working from two or more balls at once. You do not need to hold the yarn any differently. Work as though there is one strand. Do not worry if the strands twist.

attaching new yarn when shaping the neck for a pullover

When you have finished binding off one side of a neck on a V-neck or crewneck pullover, you will be instructed to attach the yarn and continue binding off on the other side of the neck. Make sure you attach the yarn in the center of the sweater and not at the outside or shoulder edge.

increasing on sleeves

You can begin to increase on sleeves on the row after the ribbing. If there is a rolled edge, you can begin after 4 rows. When the instructions tell you to increase every 4th row, this means after the first time you increase. You do not need to work 4 rows after the ribbing and then begin to increase.

This is where your increasing should occur on a stockinette sweater where you are increasing every 4th row:

Row 1: Knit—Increase
Row 2: Purl
Row 3: Knit
Row 4: Purl

Repeat rows 1–4 until the required number of increases has been worked.

striping: to cut or carry

When you are striping, you should try to carry your yarn. This means you should not cut the yarn each time you need to use a new color. You will have two or more balls of yarn hanging. If you are using more than two colors, we suggest placing the balls in plastic baggies when you are not using them. The reason to carry the yarn is that sewing the sweater together will be much easier and neater if you do. You will not have tons of ends to weave in. However, there are a few instances when you might want to cut the yarn. The first is if you do not need to use a color again for many inches. The other is if all the balls hanging are driving you mad.

choosing yarn for your sweater

For many knitters, the second most exciting part of a project is picking out the yarn. There are so many delicious new yarns on the market today, in lush colors and irresistible textures, you may feel like a kid in a candy store when you shop for yarn. We do, and we own the candy store!

We have noted the specific yarn we used for each pattern as well as the number of balls we used and the yardage. However, if you can't find the same yarn for any reason—it could be discontinued, or your shop just might not carry it—you can easily substitute yarns, as long as you choose a yarn or combination of yarns that gets the same gauge as the yarn we used.

Also, just because we used double strands of yarn doesn't necessarily mean you must. If you prefer to substitute a yarn that knits to the required gauge using a single strand, that's okay. Just be sure that when you choose a different yarn, you base the amount you will need on the yardage and not on the number of grams or balls. For example, if we use 10 balls of yarn that have 100 yards in each ball and we are knitting with a single strand of yarn, we are using 1,000 yards of yarn. If the yarn you like has 50 yards per ball, you will need 20 balls. Or, if we use 8 balls of a yarn that has 100 yards and we are using a double strand of yarn, we are using 800 yards. But if you want to use a yarn that gets the same gauge with a single strand and it has 80 yards per ball, you will need only 5 balls.

needle size

Needles come in sizes from less than 0 all the way up to 50. Your needle size helps determine your gauge (see Make a Gauge, page 41), and you need to use different size needles with different yarn weights and thicknesses. A size 0 needle has a very small diameter and is used with very, very fine yarns to make tightly textured, fine work, especially for baby clothes. A size 7 needle is a medium-size needle that is generally used with medium-weight yarn. A size 50 needle looks like a turkey baster and is used with incredibly chunky yarn or many strands knitted together at once. This produces a very thick knitted fabric.

reverse shaping

We use this term when we want you to make two pieces, one the mirror image of the other. When you shape the neck on a pullover, you bind off the center stitches and then finish one side of the sweater at a time. On one side you will have to shape the neckline in one direction (while knitting) and on the other side you will have to shape it in the other direction (while purling). Also, when you make a cardigan, you make two front sections—one that will be the right side when worn and one that will be the left side when worn—and must shape the necklines and armholes in opposite directions. The easiest way to visualize this is to shape one side without really thinking about it and then, when you get to the neck shaping on the second side, lay both pieces out as they would be on the finished sweater. You will see what the second neckline needs to look like.

how to tell if you have enough yarn for your project

It stinks to run out of yarn when you are working on the second sleeve of your sweater. Even if you choose the exact yarn and have the same stitch gauge as the pattern indicates, there are times you may need more or less yarn because the particular yarn you are using has a few extra or a few less yards per ball. Even if the difference is just a yard or two per ball, over the course of ten or fifteen balls, the yardage can really add up. Another factor that affects yardage is that your row gauge may be slightly different. If you end up knitting one extra row per every ten rows to get the same measurement as the original knitter, you'll most likely need an extra ball of yarn. Sometimes we have customers who follow our directions but need an extra ball or use one ball less. We know it is a pain to have to run back to the yarn store, but the real problem occurs if the specific color or yarn you need is no longer available.

Luckily, if you pay attention to how much yarn you are using as you knit, you can avoid these frustrations. The rule of thumb is that a sweater is broken down into thirds. You use a third of the total amount of yarn needed for the back, a third for the front, and a third for both sleeves. To determine how much yarn you are using, all you have to do is knit a ball and see how far it goes. Then divide the number of inches knit with the one ball into the length of the sweater, and that is a good estimate of how many balls you will need to knit the back. Multiply that number by three and that is how many balls you will need for the entire sweater. If the sweater has a large neck, add one extra ball. Note: A raglan sweater is broken down into quarters.

yardage

Yardage helps you determine how many balls of yarn you will need for your project. Many books and patterns tell you that you need a certain number of grams or ounces, but in our experience this is an inaccurate way to determine the amount of yarn you will need, as different fibers have different weights. Acrylic is a much lighter fiber than wool: A 50-gram ball of acrylic yarn might contain 200 yards, whereas a 50-gram ball of wool might contain only 125 yards. Therefore, if a pattern called for 200 grams of acrylic yarn and you bought 200 grams of wool instead, you would be 300 yards short. In this book, we always specify the total number of yards needed for each pattern.

increasing evenly across a row

Sometimes you need to increase across a row of ribbing to add stitches to the body of your project. This usually occurs when the stitch used on the body pulls in more than ribbing would. When making a garment that has cables, you will most likely have to add a few stitches after the edge ribbing to accommodate for this. The few times we ask you to increase stitches across a row, you should evenly space out the increase stitches over the entire width of the garment and not just cram them in at one end. We usually like to increase one stitch at the beginning, then we divide the number of stitches on the needle by the number of stitches we need to increase, which gives us a rough idea of how often we should be increasing a stitch. For example, if there are 80 stitches on the needle and we need to increase 10 stitches, we would increase every 8th stitch.

swatching

What is a swatch? It is simply knitting a small square of the pattern you are going to knit. There are two good reasons to swatch. First, it is always a good idea to make a swatch to practice a technique or stitch that you haven't done before. Get the kinks out over a small number of stitches and not the entire back of your sweater and make sure you really do understand how to cable, do a slip stitch pattern, or do a seed stitch. Second, swatching is a great way to help you choose yarn. Sometimes you may not want to knit a sweater in the suggested material or you may not be able to decide between several different yarns. A great way to decide which yarn is right for your project is to make some samples. Granted, it may cost you a few extra bucks, but we think it's worth it in order to ensure that you will end up with a sweater that you will love and wear. Remember that you will be putting a significant amount of time into the projects that you knit as well as a significant amount of money. It always pays to make sure that you are getting what you want and that you know what you are doing from the get-go.

knitting with markers

Stitch markers are very helpful when you are knitting something that consists of different stitch patterns. You can place a marker in between the two different types of stitches as a reminder that you need to change what you are doing. For example, when you are working the front of The Subway Cable, on pages 70–73, the pattern for the small size reads: K18, P2, K12, P2, K18. If you place a marker where each comma is you will always remember to switch your stitch from knit to purl. Markers are easy to use. You just place the marker onto the needle when necessary and slide it from one needle to the other on each row.

row counters

Row counters are a good gadget when you need to keep track of how many rows you have knit, usually when increasing or decreasing every few rows to create an A-line shape, a bell sleeve, or just knitting a sleeve in general. A row counter is also very helpful when you are knitting cables or need to repeat a stitch pattern every few rows. If you are using straight needles, just slide the row counter onto the end of your needle. If you are using a circular needle, just tie the counter onto your tail and then decide when you want to turn your counter—before the row or after. It is best to be consistent so that when you pick up your knitting you know whether you are about to start the row on the counter or whether you have already done that row. Just remember to turn the counter every row because, unfortunately, a counter does not turn itself. (Although it would be great if someone invented a row counter that tracked your movement and turned itself each time you finished a row, and then rewound itself whenever you ripped.) Of course, if you don't have a counter handy in a situation where you need one, the old-fashioned method of using pen and paper is always a good option—just mark off the rows you have done manually.

sleeve measurement

When knitting a sleeve, a pattern will tell you to knit until the piece measures X inches from the cast-on edge. You will then be given instructions for shaping a cap. Many knitters read this and get worried because their arms are longer than that. Let us assure you that this measurement is not the total length of the sleeve. It is the measurement up to the armpit. When shaping the cap, you will still be adding length to the sleeve. Since everyone has different length arms, our measurements are based on the average arm length. You can adjust the sleeve length by measuring from your wrist to your armpit. That is the number of inches you will want to knit before you shape the cap.

KNITTING GLOSSARY

BIND OFF (CAST OFF)
This is the way you get stitches off the needle at the end of a project. Bind off is also a method used to decrease stitches.

CAST ON
This is how you put stitches onto your needle to begin a project.

DEC.
Decrease. This is how you take stitches away once you have begun knitting. We use three methods of decreasing in this book: SSK, K2tog, and double decrease.

GARTER STITCH
Knit every row. But if you are knitting in the round (on a circular needle), then garter stitch means you should knit 1 round and purl the next.

INC.
Increase. This is how you add a stitch onto your needle once you have begun knitting. We use two methods of increasing in this book, a bar increase (Make 1, abbreviated **M1**) and knitting into the front and back of a stitch.

K
Knit.

K2TOG
Knit 2 stitches together. This is a method of decreasing. It slants your decrease toward the right.

P
Purl.

PURLWISE
This means you should move the yarn from one needle to the other as though you were going to purl the next stitch.

REV ST ST
Reverse stockinette stitch. Purl 1 row, knit 1 row, and the purl side is the right side of the garment.

RS
Right side. This is the side that will face out when you are wearing the garment.

SC
Single crochet.

SEED STITCH
Seed stitch is like a messed-up ribbing. As for ribbing, you alternate knitting and purling, but instead of knitting on the knit stitches and purling on the purl stitches to create ribs, you purl over your knit stitches and knit over your purl stitches to create little "seeds."

SSK
Slip, slip, knit. This is a method of decreasing. It slants your decrease toward the left.

ST ST
Stockinette stitch. Knit 1 row, purl 1 row. But if you are knitting in the round (on a circular needle), then St st means you should knit every round.

WS
Wrong side. This is the side that will face in when you are wearing the garment.

YARN DOUBLED
When you knit with the yarn doubled, you are working with 2 strands of yarn held together as though they were 1. Yarn tripled means working with 3 strands of yarn held together. It is no harder to knit with 2 or 3 strands of yarn than it is to knit with 1. When we tell you to use a yarn doubled or tripled, it means the yarn we used for the pattern needed to be thicker than it actually is in order to achieve the proper gauge. If you prefer not to double or triple yarn, try substituting a bulkier yarn that knits to the gauge with a single strand. Just remember that if you use a single strand of yarn where we used 2, you will need only half the yardage to complete the pattern, or one third if the yarn is tripled.

YO
Yarn over. This is how you make a hole in your work (on purpose).

★ ‧ ‧ ‧ ‧ ‧ ★
In knitting patterns, asterisks are used to indicate that a series of stitches is to be repeated. Repeat only what is between the asterisks, not what is outside of them. For example, **K2, *(K2, P2)* 3 times** means K2, K2, P2, K2, P2, K2, P2. ***(K5, K2tog)* across row** means that you should K5, K2tog, K5, K2tog, and so on across the whole row.

the yarn girls' patterns

You'll notice that there are four patterns for most basic shapes (there are three for the tees and tanks chapter). The first pattern in each category is a basic pattern. It is knit in either stockinette or garter stitch and includes only the most fundamental shaping elements. The rest of the patterns introduce you to a new, but still uncomplicated, technique. Sometimes you need to shape an A-line, follow a new stitch pattern, make a cable, or work with color. None of the new techniques are difficult to master, although some may require an extra bit of attention, at least when you begin the project.

Basic or not, for each of the patterns that follow, we provide the general instructions that tell you what type of yarn we used, its fiber content, the required gauge, and how many yards you will need. We also tell you the finished measurements for each size. We then provide directions for knitting the garment in three sizes: small, medium, and large. Step-by-step instructions that can help you with shaping A-lines, necklines, and armholes can be found in the book's appendix (pages 151–157). If you need assistance with any of the new techniques be sure to take a look at our Fundamentals and More section (pages 10–47), which provides clear and concise directions for each technique incorporated into the patterns. Also, reading our Helpful Hints (pages 41–46), will help you avoid the possible pitfalls and common mistakes.

crewneck and
funnel-neck
pullovers

Our customers love crewneck pullovers, so we often write patterns for this versatile and simple-to-knit sweater shape. Basic Instinct is perfect for beginners or for those who want to show off a beautiful yarn knit in a simple stockinette stitch. For those knitters who are ready to learn shaping, a new stitch, or want a bit more color, one of the following sweaters might be just the right thing. Indulge Yourself is a sophisticated yet whimsical funnel-neck. Decreases on the sleeves create a bell shape, which complements the body's A-line shape. We knit it in cashmere, but you can knit it in any yarn that gets the same gauge. Beware the Bunny is the perfect introduction to intarsia. This fun-to-make sweater is knit with only two colors at a time, so bobbins are not needed. Choosing the colors for this sweater is half the fun of making it, but the design itself makes a statement if you only want to knit it in one color. Cables in Chamonix is a slightly fitted sweater with a soft look. The cable and rib stitch are of the most basic variety and a great introduction to this technique. Whether you want a basic crewneck, a cowl neck, or a turtleneck, we've got you covered.

A lot of people want to make a "basic" sweater that is easy to knit, is totally versatile, and can be dressed up or down. Many end up making a crewneck pullover, finding it's the yarn that turns a basic shaped sweater into something special. You'll know instinctively when you spot the perfect yarn for your "not so basic" sweater. This sweater with its classic style looks great at the grocery store and even better on Broadway!

basic instinct

BACK:

With #7 needle, cast on 78 (86, 94) stitches. Work in K1, P1 ribbing for 6 rows. Change to #9 needle and work in St st until piece measures 11.5" (13", 14") from the cast-on edge, ending with a WS row. SHAPE ARMHOLES: Bind off 4 stitches at the beginning of the next 2 rows. Bind off 3 stitches at the beginning of the following 2 rows. Then decrease 1 stitch at each edge every other row 2 (3, 5) times until 60 (66, 70) stitches remain. *(See step-by-step instructions on page 151.)* Continue working in St st until piece measures 19.5" (21.5", 23") from cast-on edge, ending with a WS row. Bind off all stitches loosely.

FRONT:

Work as for back until piece measures 11.5" (13", 14") from cast-on edge, ending with a WS row. SHAPE ARM-HOLES: Bind off 4 stitches at the beginning of the next 2 rows. Bind off 3 stitches at the beginning of the following 2 rows. Then decrease 1 stitch at each edge every other row 2 (3, 5) times until 60 (66, 70) stitches remain. *(See step-by-step instructions on page 151.)* Continue working in St st until piece measures 17" (19", 20.5") from cast-on edge, ending with a WS row. SHAPE CREW NECK: Bind off center 18 (20, 22) stitches and then begin working each side of the neck separately. At the beginning of each neck edge, every other row, bind off 3 stitches 1 time, 2 stitches 1 time, 1 stitch 2 times. *(See step-by-step instructions on page 151.)* Continue to work on remaining 14 (16, 17) stitches with no further decreasing until piece measures 19.5" (21.5", 23") from cast-on edge, ending with a WS row. Bind off all stitches loosely.

SLEEVES:

With #7 needle, cast on 38 (40, 42) stitches. Work in K1, P1 ribbing for 6 rows. Change to #9 needle and work in St st. **At the same time,** increase 1 stitch at each edge every 8th row 10 times until you have 58 (60, 62) stitches.

Note: Increase leaving 2 edge stitches on either side. This means you should knit 2 stitches, increase a stitch, knit to the last 2 stitches, increase a stitch, and then knit the remaining 2 stitches. Increasing like this makes it easier to sew up your seams.

When sleeve measures 17.5" (18.5", 19.5") from cast-on edge, ending with a WS row, SHAPE CAP: Bind off 4 stitches at the beginning of the next 2 rows. Bind off 3 stitches at the beginning of the following 2 rows. Then decrease 1 stitch at each edge, every other row 2 (3, 5) times. Bind off 2 stitches at the beginning of the next 14 rows until 12 (12, 10) stitches remain. Bind off all stitches loosely.

FINISHING:

Sew shoulder seams together. Sew sleeves on. Sew up side and sleeve seams. (For more detailed directions, see Finishing Techniques, page 29.) With circular 16" #7 needle, pick up 74 (78, 80) stitches around the neck and work in K1, P1 ribbing for 6 rows to make crewneck. Bind off all stitches loosely.

YARN: Tahki, New Tweed (103 yards / 50g ball)
FIBER CONTENT: 70% Merino Wool / 15% Silk / 11% Cotton / 4% Viscose
COLOR: 12
AMOUNT: 8 (10, 12) balls
TOTAL YARDAGE: 824 (1030, 1236) yards
GAUGE: 4.5 stitches = 1 inch; 18 stitches = 4 inches
NEEDLE SIZE: US 9 (5.5mm) or size needed to obtain gauge; US 7 (4.5mm) for edge ribbing; circular 16" US 7 (4.5mm) for neck ribbing
SIZES: S (M, L)
KNITTED MEASUREMENTS: Width = 17" (19", 21"); Length = 19.5" (21.5", 23"); Sleeve Length = 17.5" (18.5", 19.5")

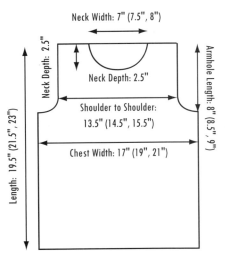

Neck Width: 7" (7.5", 8")
Neck Depth: 2.5"
Neck Depth: 2.5"
Armhole Length: 8" (8.5", 9")
Shoulder to Shoulder: 13.5" (14.5", 15.5")
Chest Width: 17" (19", 21")
Length: 19.5" (21.5", 23")

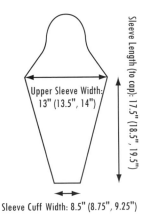

Sleeve Length (to cap): 17.5" (18.5", 19.5")
Upper Sleeve Width: 13" (13.5", 14")
Sleeve Cuff Width: 8.5" (8.75", 9.25")

indulge yourself

Sometimes you see a sweater and know you just have to have it. This happened to Edie while she was shopping at a Manhattan boutique. Undeterred by the laughable price tag, she made a quick sketch of the sweater. She then came directly to our store, chose a luxurious cashmere yarn, and had us write a pattern. The A-line shaping and the funky cowl neck looked great on her and is a wonderful indulgence when knit in cashmere. This sweater also looks great knit in other yarns, just be sure you get the same gauge.

YARN: Classic Elite, Forbidden
(65 yards / 50g ball)
FIBER CONTENT: 100% Cashmere
COLOR: 60292
AMOUNT: 9 (10, 12) balls
TOTAL YARDAGE: 585 (650, 780) yards
GAUGE: **Stitch Gauge:** 2.75 stitches =
1 inch; 11 stitches = 4 inches
        Row Gauge: 3.75 rows = 1 inch;
15 rows = 4 inches
NEEDLE SIZE: US 13 (9mm) or size
needed to obtain gauge
SIZES: S (M, L)
KNITTED MEASUREMENTS: Width =
15.5″ (17.5″, 19″); Length = 20″ (22″, 24″);
Sleeve Length = 19″ (20″, 21″)

BACK & FRONT:

With #13 needle, cast on 58 (66, 72)
stitches. Work in St st for 6 rows.
SHAPE A-LINE: Continue in St st,
decreasing 1 stitch at each end every 6th
row 8 (9, 10) times until 42 (48, 52)
stitches remain. *(See step-by-step
instructions on page 151.)* Continue in
St st with no further shaping until piece
measures 12″ (13.5″, 15″) from cast-on
edge, ending with a WS row. **SHAPE
RAGLAN:** Bind off 2 stitches at the
beginning of the next 2 rows. Then
decrease 1 stitch at each edge every
other row 12 (14, 16) times until 14 (16, 16)
stitches remain. *(See step-by-step
instructions on page 151.)* **SHAPE
FUNNEL NECK:** Work in reverse
St st on remaining 14 (16, 16) stitches,
increasing 1 stitch at each end
of every 4th row 8 times until you have
30 (32, 32) stitches. *(See step-by-step
instructions on page 151.)* Bind off all
stitches loosely.

SLEEVES:

With #13 needle, cast on 36 (40, 44)
stitches. Work in St st, decreasing 1
stitch at each end every other row 7
(8, 9) times until 22 (24, 26) stitches
remain. Then continue in St st, increasing 1 stitch at each end every 10th row 4
times until you have 30 (32, 34) stitches.
Then increase 1 stitch at each end every
4th row 3 (4, 5) times until you have 36
(40, 44) stitches. *Note: Increase leaving 2
edge stitches on either side. This means
you should knit 2 stitches, increase a
stitch, knit to the last 2 stitches, increase
a stitch, and then knit the remaining 2
stitches. Increasing like this makes it
easier to sew up your seams.* When
sleeve measures 19″ (20″, 21″) from cast-
on edge, end with a WS row. **SHAPE
RAGLAN:** Bind off 2 stitches at the
beginning of the next 2 rows. Then
decrease 1 stitch at each edge every
other row 12 (14, 16) times until 8 stitches
remain. *(See step-by-step instructions
on page 151.)* Continue in reverse St st on
remaining 8 stitches for 32 rows. Bind off
all stitches loosely.

FINISHING:

Sew raglan seams together. Sew sleeve
and side seams. Sew up neck seams so
that St st side is the RS. (For more
detailed directions, see Finishing
Techniques, page 29.)

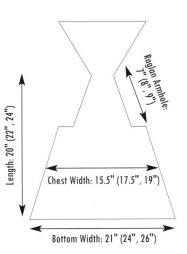

Raglan Armhole: 7″ (8″, 9″)

Length: 20″ (22″, 24″)

Chest Width: 15.5″ (17.5″, 19″)

Bottom Width: 21″ (24″, 26″)

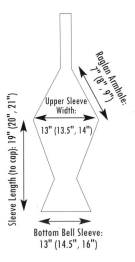

Raglan Armhole: 7″ (8″, 9″)

Upper Sleeve Width: 13″ (13.5″, 14″)

Sleeve Length (to cap): 19″ (20″, 21″)

Bottom Bell Sleeve: 13″ (14.5″, 16″)

beware the bunny

Helen was obsessed with learning intarsia, a form of color knitting. She liked the sound of the word and wanted to be able to say she'd mastered the technique. She searched for the perfect pattern, but all she could find were goofy motifs. We suggested this simple sweater with color blocks as a funky entrée to this new technique. She chose a wonderful color combination and ended up with a sophisticated sweater instead of one with a large bunny or a daisy in the center.

BACK & FRONT:

With #11 needle and color A, cast on 56
(64, 70) stitches. Then work in St st as
follows:

Row 1: K28 (32, 35) stitches with color A
and K28 (32, 35) stitches with color B.

Row 2: P28 (32, 35) stitches with color B
and P28 (32, 35) stitches with color A.
Continue working in St st in the established color pattern with colors A & B for
7.5″ (8″, 8.5″) from cast-on edge, ending
with a WS row. Cut A & B.

Then work in St st as follows:

Row 1: K28 (32, 35) stitches with color C
and K28 (32, 35) stitches with color A.

Row 2: P28 (32, 35) stitches with color A
and P28 (32, 35) stitches with color C.
Continue in St st in the established color
pattern until piece measures 14″ (15″,
16″) from the cast-on edge, ending with a
WS row. SHAPE ARMHOLES: Bind
off 3 stitches at the beginning of the next
2 rows. Bind off 2 stitches at the beginning of the following 2 rows. Then
decrease 1 stitch at each edge every
other row 4 (6, 6) times until 38 (42, 48)
stitches remain. *(See step-by-step
instructions on page 151.)* **At the same
time,** when piece measures 14.5″ (15.5″,
16.5″) from cast-on edge, ending with a
WS row, cut C & A. Begin knitting with A
& B again, switching colors in the middle
as set.

When you are finished shaping the armhole decreases, continue working in St st
on 19 (21, 24) stitches A and 19 (21, 24)
stitches B until piece measures 22.5″
(24″, 25.5″) from cast-on edge, ending
with a WS row. SHAPE FUNNEL
NECK: Bind off 8 (10, 12) stitches at
beginning of next 2 rows. *(See step-by-
step instructions on page 151.)* Continue
working in St st on 11 (11, 12) stitches A

and 11 (11, 12) stitches B for 6
more rows. Bind off all stitches
loosely in A & B.

SLEEVES:

*Note: Work color C for first 11″
(11.5″, 12.5″) then continue in
color A until sleeve is complete.*

With #11 needle and color C, cast on 26
(28, 32) stitches. Work in St st. **At the
same time,** increase 1 stitch at each edge
every 6th row 8 (9, 10) times until you
have 42 (46, 52) stitches. *Note: Increase
leaving 2 edge stitches on either side.
This means you should knit 2 stitches,
increase a stitch, knit to the last 2
stitches, increase a stitch, and then knit
the remaining 2 stitches. Increasing like
this makes it easier to sew up your
seams.* When sleeve measures 17″ (18″,
19.5″) from cast-on edge, ending with a
WS row, SHAPE CAP: Bind off 3
stitches at the beginning of the next 2
rows. Bind off 2 stitches at the beginning
of the following 2 rows. Then decrease 1
stitch at each edge every other row 4 (6,
6) times. Bind off 2 stitches at the beginning of the next 10 (10, 12) rows until 4
(4, 6) stitches remain. Bind off all
stitches loosely.

FINISHING:

Sew shoulder seams together. Sew
sleeves on. Sew up side and sleeve
seams. (For more detailed instructions,
see Finishing Techniques, page 29.)

YARN: Rowan, Polar
(109 yards / 100g ball)
FIBER CONTENT: 60% Wool / 30%
Alpaca / 10% Acrylic
COLORS: A: 647; B: 640; C: 653
AMOUNT: A: 3 (4, 4) balls; B: 2 (3, 3)
balls; C: 2 (2, 2) balls
TOTAL YARDAGE: 763 (981, 981) yards
GAUGE: 3 stitches = 1 inch;
12 stitches = 4 inches
NEEDLE SIZE: US 11 (8mm) or size
needed to obtain gauge
SIZES: S (M, L)
KNITTED MEASUREMENTS: Width =
18.5″ (21″, 23″); Length = 22.5″ (24″,
25.5″); Sleeve Length = 17″ (18″, 19.5″)

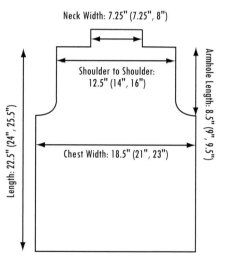

Neck Width: 7.25″ (7.25″, 8″)

Shoulder to Shoulder:
12.5″ (14″, 16″)

Armhole Length: 8.5″ (9″, 9.5″)

Length: 22.5″ (24″, 25.5″)

Chest Width: 18.5″ (21″, 23″)

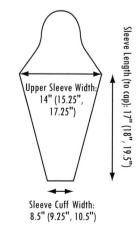

Upper Sleeve Width:
14″ (15.25″,
17.25″)

Sleeve Length (to cap): 17″ (18″, 19.5″)

Sleeve Cuff Width:
8.5″ (9.25″, 10.5″)

cables in chamonix

Celeste needed a ski sweater for an upcoming trip to the Alps for a ski vacation in Chamonix. She wanted cables and a turtleneck but did not want to end up with a theme sweater, specifically "no reindeers and no Christmas trees." We chose this beautiful, soft yarn and designed a slightly fitted cable sweater. It turned out great, and we have a picture of Celeste in the sweater snuggling up to a very cute Frenchman to prove it.

CABLE PATTERN:

C6B = Place 3 stitches on a cable needle, hold them at the back of work. Knit 3 stitches from the left needle, knit 3 stitches from the cable needle.

BACK:

With #10.5 needle, cast on 64 (72, 80) stitches. Work in pattern as follows:

Row 1: K9 (13, 11) *P2, K6, P2, K2* 3 (3, 4) times, end P2, K6, P2, K9 (13, 11).

Rows 2, 4, 6, 8 & 10: P9 (13, 11) *K2, P6, K2, P2* 3 (3, 4) times, end K2, P6, K2, P9 (13, 11).

Row 3: K9 (13, 11) *P2, C6B, P2, K2* 3 (3, 4) times, end P2, C6B, P2, K9 (13, 11)

Rows 5, 7 & 9: As row 1.

Repeat this 10-row pattern until piece measures 13.5″ (14.5″, 16″) from the cast-on edge, ending with a WS row. S H A P E A R M H O L E S : Bind off 3 stitches at the beginning of the next 2 rows. Bind off 2 stitches at the beginning of the following 2 rows. Then decrease 1 stitch at each edge every other row 2 (3, 4) times until 50 (56, 62) stitches remain. *(See step-by-step instructions on page 151.)* Continue working in pattern until piece measures 21.5″ (23″, 25″) from cast-on edge, ending with a WS row. Bind off all stitches loosely.

FRONT:

Work as for back until piece measures 13.5″ (14.5″, 16″) from cast-on edge, ending with a WS row. S H A P E A R M H O L E S : Bind off 3 stitches at the beginning of the next 2 rows. Bind off 2 stitches at the beginning of the following 2 rows. Then decrease 1 stitch at each edge every other row 2 (3, 4) times until 50 (56, 62) stitches remain. *(See step-by-step instructions on page 151.)* Continue working in pattern until piece measures 19″ (20.5″, 22.5″) from cast-on edge, ending with a WS row. S H A P E C R E W N E C K : Bind off center 6 stitches and then begin working each side of the neck separately. At the beginning of each neck

edge, every other row, bind off 4 stitches 1 time, 3 stitches 1 time, 2 stitches 1 time, 1 stitch 1 (2, 3) time. *(See step-by-step instructions on page 152.)* Continue to work on remaining 12 (14, 16) stitches with no further decreasing until piece measures 21.5″ (23″, 25″) from cast-on edge, ending with a WS row. Bind off all stitches loosely.

SLEEVES:

With #10.5 needle, cast on 32 (36, 40) stitches. Work in pattern as follows:

Row 1: K7 (9, 11), P2, K2, P2, K6, P2, K2, P2, K7 (9, 11).

Rows 2, 4, 6, 8 & 10: P7 (9, 11), K2, P2, K2, P6, K2, P2, K2, P7 (9, 11).

Row 3: K7 (9, 11), P2, K2, P2, C6B, P2, K2, P2, K7 (9, 11).

Rows 5, 7 & 9: As row 1.

Repeat this 10-row pattern and **at the same time,** increase 1 stitch at each edge every 8th row 8 (8, 9) times until you have 48 (52, 58) stitches. *Note: Increase leaving 2 edge stitches on either side. This means you should knit 2 stitches, increase a stitch, knit to the last 2 stitches, increase a stitch, and then knit the remaining 2 stitches. Increasing like this makes it easier to sew up your seams.* Remember as you increase stitches the number of knits and purls at the beginning and end of the row will also increase. When sleeve measures 17″ (18″, 19.5″) from cast-on edge, ending with a WS row, S H A P E C A P : Bind off 3 stitches at the beginning of the next 2 rows. Bind off 2 stitches at the beginning of the following 2 rows. Then decrease 1 stitch at each edge every other row 2 (3, 4) times. Bind off 2 stitches at the beginning of the next 14 (14, 16) rows until 6 (8, 8) stitches remain. Bind off all stitches loosely.

FINISHING:

Sew shoulder seams together. Sew sleeves on. Sew up side and sleeve seams. (For more detailed instructions,

YARN: GGH, Savannah (84 yards / 50g ball)
FIBER CONTENT: 43% Alpaca / 23% Linen / 19% Wool / 15% Polyamide
COLOR: 3
AMOUNT: 8 (9, 11) balls
TOTAL YARDAGE: 672 (756, 924) yards
GAUGE: 3.5 stitches = 1 inch; 14 stitches = 4 inches (in stockinette stitch)
NEEDLE SIZE: US 10.5 (7mm) or size needed to obtain gauge; circular 16″ US 10.5 (7mm) for neck ribbing
SIZES: S (M, L)
KNITTED MEASUREMENTS: Width = 16″ (18″, 20″); Length = 21.5″ (23″, 25″); Sleeve Length = 17″ (18″, 19.5″)

see Finishing Techniques, page 29.) With circular 16″ #10.5 needle, pick up 64 (64, 68) stitches around the neck and work in K2, P2 ribbing for 8″. Bind off all stitches loosely.

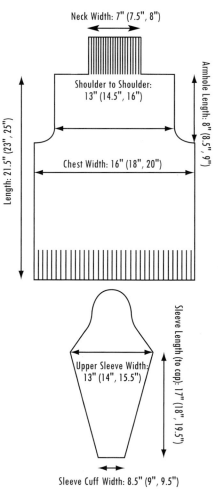

Neck Width: 7″ (7.5″, 8″)

Shoulder to Shoulder: 13″ (14.5″, 16″)

Armhole Length: 8″ (8.5″, 9″)

Length: 21.5″ (23″, 25″)

Chest Width: 16″ (18″, 20″)

Upper Sleeve Width: 13″ (14″, 15.5″)

Sleeve Length (to cap): 17″ (18″, 19.5″)

Sleeve Cuff Width: 8.5″ (9″, 9.5″)

v-neck pullovers

Unlike crewneck sweaters, the shaping for V-necks begins lower down and there is no center bind off, just single decreases up the length of the neck of the sweater. When making a set-in sleeve or raglan-sleeve sweater, the V-neck shaping can become a bit tricky because you need to work the decreases for the armhole at the same time as the V-neck. All this requires is a little extra concentration or some simple note-keeping. The Soccer Mom Sweater lets you practice working both decreases at the same time without having to think about anything else. It is made with a super chunky yarn and is the perfect project for beginners or more advanced knitters who want to knit up a V-neck in a jiffy. Even Daniele Did It, Yet Again uses the technique intarsia to knit a vertical stripe down the front of the sweater. Intarsia is simple, you just have to twist the colors correctly to lock them, but be careful that the yarn doesn't tangle. The Subway Cable has a chunky cable going up the center of the front that is separated from the stockinette stitch by two purl stitches on either side. The cable splits at the V, and the decreases for the neck are worked so that no finishing is required. Not Your Standard-Issue Sweatshirt, Take Two incorporates cables and seed stitch. The cables are straightforward and the seed stitch is just a simple K1, P1, which is a snap to master if you can identify a knit stitch from a purl stitch.

soccer mom sweater

The mother of three boys, Lisa spends a great deal of her time at soccer practice, at baseball games, and at the ice rink. She loves spending time with her kids and being a part of their activities, but to be honest, she gets a little antsy just sitting there watching. Reading wasn't an option because she needs to be able to see the goals scored and home runs hit. Jordana, her sister-in-law, suggested she knit because "it is the perfect portable hobby that lets you still be involved in whatever is going on around you." Jordana taught Lisa to knit that very afternoon. After making a scarf or two, Lisa wanted to make a simple V-neck pullover sweater. She made this one during three soccer practices, two baseball games, and a hockey game or two—it is the perfect project to keep the hands busy while the brain may be otherwise occupied.

YARN: Tahki, Bianca
(35 yards / 50g ball)
FIBER CONTENT: 100% Wool
COLOR: 06
AMOUNT: 11 (13, 15) balls
TOTAL YARDAGE: 385 (455, 525) yards
GAUGE: 2 stitches = 1 inch;
8 stitches = 4 inches
NEEDLE SIZE: US 17 (12mm) or size needed to obtain gauge; US 15 (10mm) for ribbing; circular 16" US 15 (10mm) for neck ribbing
SIZES: S (M, L)
KNITTED MEASUREMENTS: Width = 18" (20", 23"); Length = 20" (22", 25"); Sleeve Length = 17" (18", 19")

BACK:

With #15 needle, cast on 36 (40, 46) stitches. Work in K2, P2 ribbing for 6 rows as follows:

For Small & Medium: K2, P2 every row.

For Large:

Row 1: K2 *(P2, K2)* to end.

Row 2: P2 *(K2, P2)* to end.

Repeat rows 1 & 2 twice more.

For all sizes: Change to #17 needle and work in St st until piece measures 11.5" (13", 15") from cast-on edge, ending with a WS row. **SHAPE ARMHOLES:** Bind off 2 stitches at the beginning of the next 2 rows. Then decrease 1 stitch at

each edge every other row 3 (4, 5) times until 26 (28, 32) stitches remain. *(See step-by-step instructions on page 152.)* Continue working in St st until piece measures 20" (22", 25") from cast-on edge, ending with a WS row. Bind off all stitches loosely.

FRONT:

Note: You may be shaping the armhole and the V-neck at the same time. Please read the instructions before proceeding.

Work as for back until piece measures 11.5″ (13″, 15″) from cast-on edge, ending with a WS row. S H A P E A R M H O L E S : Bind off 2 stitches at the beginning of the next 2 rows. Then decrease 1 stitch at each edge every other row 3 (4, 5) times until 26 (28, 32) stitches remain. *(See step-by-step instructions on page 152.)* Continue working in St st until piece measures 13″ (14″, 15.5″) from cast-on edge, ending with a WS row. S H A P E V - N E C K : Place a marker at the center.

Row 1: Knit until 4 stitches before the marker, K2tog, K2. Turn work around as though you were at the end of the row. You are going to ignore the rest of the stitches.

Rows 2 & 4: Purl.

Row 3: Knit.

Repeat rows 1 through 4 twice more until 10 (11, 13) stitches remain. Then repeat rows 1 & 2 3 (4, 5) times until 7 (7, 8) stitches remain. Continue to work on these stitches until piece measures 20″ (22″, 25″) from cast-on edge, ending with a WS row. *(See step-by-step instructions on page 152.)* Bind off all stitches loosely.

Attach yarn to other side. You should be on a RS row.

Row 1: K2, SSK, knit until end.

Rows 2 & 4: Purl.

Row 3: Knit.

Repeat rows 1 through 4 twice more until 10 (11, 13) stitches remain. Then repeat rows 1 & 2 3 (4, 5) more times until 7 (7, 8) stitches remain. Continue to work on these stitches until piece measures 20″ (22″, 25″) from cast-on edge, ending with a WS row. *(See step-by-step instructions on page 152.)* Bind off all stitches loosely.

SLEEVES:

With #15 needle, cast on 18 (20, 22) stitches. Work in K2, P2 ribbing for 6 rows as follows:

For Small & Large:

Row 1: K2 *(P2, K2)* to end.

Row 2: P2 *(K2, P2)* to end.

Repeat rows 1 & 2 twice more.

For Medium: K2, P2 every row.

For all sizes: Change to #17 needle and work in St st. **At the same time,** increase 1 stitch at each edge every 8th row 6 (6, 7) times until you have 30 (32, 36) stitches. *Note: Increase leaving 2 edge stitches on either side of work. This means you should knit 2 stitches, increase a stitch, knit to the last 2 stitches, increase a stitch, and then knit the remaining 2 stitches. Increasing like this makes it easier to sew up your seams.* When sleeve measures 17″ (18″, 19″) from cast-on edge, ending with a WS row, S H A P E C A P : Bind off 2 stitches at the beginning of the next 2 rows. Then decrease 1 stitch at each edge every other row 3 (4, 5) times. Bind off 2 stitches at the beginning of the next 6 rows until 8 (8, 10) stitches remain. Bind off all stitches loosely.

FINISHING:

Sew shoulder seams together. Sew sleeves on. Sew down side and sleeve seams. (For more detailed instructions, see Finishing Techniques, page 29.) With 16″ #15 circular needle and RS facing you, pick up 14 (18, 18) stitches across the back neck, 20 (22, 24) stitches down the left front, 1 stitch in the center of the V, and 20 (22, 24) stitches up the right neck. You should have 55 (63, 67) stitches. Work in K2, P2 ribbing, keeping the center stitch as a knit 1 and decreasing 1 stitch before the knit 1 by doing a K2tog and 1 stitch after the knit 1 by doing an SSK. Work 2 rows in the ribbing with the decreases and then bind off all stitches loosely.

Note: If you end with a K2 before the center stitch, begin with a K2 up the right side. If you end with a P2 before the center stitch, begin with a P2 up the right side.

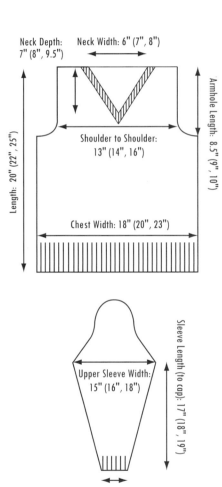

Neck Depth:
7" (8", 9.5")

Neck Width: 6" (7", 8")

Length: 20" (22", 25")

Shoulder to Shoulder:
13" (14", 16")

Armhole Length: 8.5" (9", 10")

Chest Width: 18" (20", 23")

Upper Sleeve Width:
15" (16", 18")

Sleeve Length (to cap): 17" (18", 19")

Sleeve Cuff Width: 9" (10", 11")

even daniele did it,
yet again

Daniele's knitting skills have come a long way since her days of uneven sleeves and too-low necklines. Her first true successes were bulky funnel-necks, then, as her confidence as a knitter grew, she made a simple striped baby sweater—and now after completing this sweater, she has mastered intarsia! Daniele wanted to make a sweater with a vertical stripe down the center, "for a kind of vintage look," she said. We designed this sweater for her and held our breath as she walked out the door with a bag full of yarn and a five-minute primer on color knitting. She came back to the Yarn Company a few weeks later with a big smile on her face. She unbuttoned her jacket and said, "Look, I did it again."

YARN: Filatura Di Crosa, Zara Plus (77 yards / 50g ball)
FIBER CONTENT: 100% Merino Wool
COLORS: A: 18; B: 17
AMOUNT: A: 9 (10, 11) balls; B: 1 ball
TOTAL YARDAGE: A: 693 (770, 847) yards; B: 77 yards
GAUGE: **Stitch Gauge:** 4 stitches = 1 inch; 16 stitches = 4 inches
     Row Gauge: 5.5 rows = 1 inch; 22 rows = 4 inches
NEEDLE SIZE: US 10 (6mm) or size needed to obtain gauge; circular 16″ US 8 (5mm) for neck ribbing
SIZES: S (M, L)
KNITTED MEASUREMENTS: Width = 17″ (19″, 21″); Length = 20″ (22″, 24″); Sleeve Length = 19″ (20″, 21″)

BACK:

With #10 needle and color A, cast on 68 (76, 84) stitches. Work in K2, P2 ribbing for 6 rows.

Work in St st until piece measures 12″ (13″, 14″) from cast-on edge, ending with a WS row.

SHAPE RAGLAN ARMHOLES:

Bind off 2 (3, 3) stitches at the beginning of the next 2 rows. Then decrease 1 stitch at each edge every other row 20 (22, 25) times until 24 (26, 28) stitches remain. *(See step-by-step instructions on page 152.)* Bind off all stitches loosely.

FRONT:

Note: When working the front it is easiest to use 3 separate balls: 1 ball in the center for the stripe and 2 separate balls of the main color on either side.

With #10 needle and color A, cast on 68 (76, 84) stitches. Work in K2, P2 ribbing for 6 rows.

Work in St st as follows:

Row 1: Knit 28 (32, 36) stitches with color A, 12 stitches with color B, 28 (32, 36) stitches with color A.

Row 2: Purl 28 (32, 36) stitches with color A, 12 stitches with color B, 28 (32, 36) stitches with color A.

Continue working in this color pattern until piece measures 12″ (13″, 14″) from cast-on edge, ending with a WS row.

SHAPE RAGLAN ARMHOLES:

Bind off 2 (3, 3) stitches at the beginning of the next 2 rows. Then decrease 1 stitch at each edge every other row 4 (4, 5) times until 56 (62, 68) stitches remain. *(See step-by-step instructions on page 152.)*

SHAPE V-NECK and RAGLAN ARMHOLE at the same time as follows: Place a marker on the needle to indicate the center of the work. Work 1 side at a time.

Note: Work in the intarsia pattern until there are no stitches remaining in Color B.

Row 1: K2, SSK, knit to 2 stitches before the marker, K2tog.

Row 2: Purl.

Row 3: K2, SSK, knit to end.

Row 4: Purl.

Repeat rows 1 through 4 until you have completed row 36 (40, 44). Proceed as follows:

Row 37 (41, 45): K2, SSK, K2tog, K2 (6 stitches remain).

Row 38 (42, 46): Purl.

Row 39 (43, 47): K1, SSK, K2tog, K1 (4 stitches remain).

Row 40 (44, 48): Purl.

Row 41 (45, 49): SSK, K2tog (2 stitches remain).

Row 42 (46, 50): P2tog.

Pull yarn through the remaining loop and fasten.

Attach yarn to the other side of the V and repeat the decrease sequence making the following changes:

Row 1: SSK, knit until the last 4 stitches, K2tog, K2.

Row 3: Knit until the last 4 stitches, K2tog, K2.

SLEEVES:

With #10 needle and color A, cast on 26 (30, 34) stitches. Work in K2, P2 ribbing for 6 rows as follows:

Row 1: K2 *(P2, K2)*.

Row 2: P2 *(K2, P2)*.

Then work in St st. **At the same time,** increase 1 stitch at each edge every 8th row 12 (13, 15) times until you have 50 (56, 64) stitches.

Note: Increase leaving 2 edge stitches on either side of work. This means you should knit 2 stitches, increase a stitch, knit to the last 2 stitches, increase a stitch, and then knit the remaining 2 stitches. Increasing like this makes it easier to sew up your seams.

Continue working in St st until sleeve measures 19" (20", 21") from cast-on edge, ending with a WS row. SHAPE RAGLAN SLEEVE: Bind off 2 (3, 3) stitches at the beginning of the next 2 rows. Then decrease 1 stitch at each edge every other row 20 (22, 25) times until 6 (6, 8) stitches remain. Bind off all stitches loosely.

FINISHING:

Sew raglan seams together. Sew down side and sleeve seams. (For more detailed instructions, see Finishing Techniques, page 29.) With circular 16" #8 needle and color B and RS facing you, pick up 22 (26, 26) stitches across the back neck, 4 stitches down left sleeve, 32 (34, 36) stitches down the left neck, 2 stitches in the center of the V, 32 (34, 36) stitches up the right neck, and 4 stitches across the right sleeve. You will have a total of 96 (104, 108) stitches. Work in K2, P2 ribbing, keeping the center 2 stitches as a K2 and decreasing 1 stitch before the K2 by doing a K2tog and 1 stitch after the K2 by doing an SSK. Work 5 rows in the ribbing with the decreases and then bind off all stitches loosely.

Note: If you end with a K2 before the center stitches, begin with a K2 up the right side. If you end with a P2 before the center stitches, begin with a P2 up the right side.

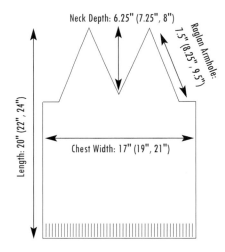

Neck Depth: 6.25" (7.25", 8")

Raglan Armhole: 7.5" (8.25", 9.5")

Length: 20" (22", 24")

Chest Width: 17" (19", 21")

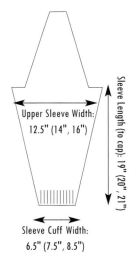

Upper Sleeve Width: 12.5" (14", 16")

Sleeve Length (to cap): 19" (20", 21")

Sleeve Cuff Width: 6.5" (7.5", 8.5")

the subway cable

Karen wanted an easy cable pattern that wasn't too busy, too difficult, or just too traditional looking. "I need something I can knit on the subway," she said. This sweater with the one large cable up the front was her answer. Karen learned to cable without any hassle (she only used her cable needle five times). She chose a wonderful combination of yarns, a kid mohair and a hand-dyed worsted yarn, to make this beautiful sweater.

YARNS: A: Manos Del Uruguay (138 yards / 100g ball); B: GGH Soft Kid (145 yards / 25g ball)
FIBER CONTENT: A: 100% Handspun Pure Wool; B: 70% Super Kid Mohair / 25% Polyamide / 5% Wool
COLORS: A: 30; B: 67
AMOUNT: A: 4 (5, 6) balls; B: 4 (5, 6) balls
TOTAL YARDAGE: A: 552 (690, 828) yards; B: 580 (725, 870) yards
GAUGE: 3 stitches = 1 inch; 12 stitches = 4 inches
NEEDLE SIZE: US 13 (9mm) or size needed to obtain gauge; US 11 (8mm) for ribbing
SIZES: S (M, L)
KNITTED MEASUREMENTS: Width = 17" (19", 22"); Length = 20.5" (22", 25"); Sleeve Length = 17" (18", 19.5")
Yarn is worked double throughout the sweater—this means you should hold 1 strand of A and 1 strand of B together as though they are 1.

PATTERN STITCH:

C12B = Place 6 stitches on cable needle; hold at the back of the work. Knit 6 from the left needle, then knit 6 from the cable needle.

BACK:

With #11 needle and 1 strand of yarn A and 1 strand of yarn B, cast on 52 (58, 66) stitches. Work in K2, P2 ribbing for 6 rows as follows:

For Small: (K2, P2)* to end.

For Medium & Large:

Row 1: K2, *(P2, K2)* to end.

Row 2: P2, *(K2, P2)* to end.

For all sizes: Change to #13 needle and work in St st until piece measures 12.5" (13.5", 15.5") from cast-on edge, ending with a WS row. SHAPE ARMHOLES: Bind off 3 stitches at the beginning of the next 2 rows. Next, bind off 2 stitches at the beginning of the following 2 rows. Then decrease 1 stitch at each edge every other row 3 (3, 5) times until 36 (42, 46) stitches remain. *(See step-by-step instructions on page 152.)* Continue working in St st until piece measures 20.5" (22", 25") from cast-on edge, ending with a WS row. Bind off all stitches loosely.

FRONT:

Note: You may be shaping the armhole and the V-neck at the same time. Please read the instructions before proceeding.

Work as for back until you have completed 6 rows of ribbing. Change to #13 needle and work cable pattern as follows:

Row 1: K18 (21, 25), P2, K12, P2, K18 (21, 25).

Row 2 & all even rows: P18 (21, 25), K2, P12, K2, P18 (21, 25).

Row 3: K18 (21, 25), P2, C12B, P2, K18 (21, 25).

Rows 5, 7, 9 & 11: Work as row 1.

Repeat this 12-row pattern for the front until piece measures 12.5" (13.5", 15.5") from cast-on edge, ending with a WS row. SHAPE ARMHOLES: Bind off 3 stitches at the beginning of the next 2 rows. Bind off 2 stitches at the beginning of the following 2 rows. Then decrease 1 stitch at each edge every other row 3 (3, 5) times until 36 (42, 46) stitches remain. *(See step-by-step instructions on page 152.)* Continue in St st until piece measures 14.5″ (15″, 16.5″) from cast-on edge, ending with a WS row.

Note: Try to begin the V shaping shortly after you do a cable—on a row 5, 7, or 9. This may mean you begin the V a little lower or higher.

SHAPE V-NECK: Place a marker at the center.

Row 1: Knit until 10 stitches before the marker, K2tog, P2, K6. Turn work around as though you were at the end of the row. You are going to ignore the rest of the stitches.

Row 2: P6, K2, purl to end of row.

Repeat rows 1 & 2 7 (8, 9) more times until 10 (12, 13) stitches remain. *(See step-by-step instructions on page 152.)* Continue to work on these stitches until piece measures 20.5″ (22″, 25″) from cast-on edge, ending with a WS row. Bind off all stitches loosely.

Attach yarn to other side. You should be on a RS row.

Row 1: K6, P2, SSK, knit until end.

Row 2: Purl until 8 stitches remain, K2, P6.

Repeat rows 1 & 2 7 (8, 9) more times until 10 (12, 13) stitches remain. *(See step-by-step instructions on page 152.)* Continue to work on these stitches until piece measures 20.5″ (22″, 25″) from cast-on edge, ending with a WS row. Bind off all stitches loosely.

SLEEVES:

With #11 needle and 1 strand of yarn A and 1 strand of yarn B, cast on 30 (32, 34) stitches. Work in K2, P2 ribbing for 6 rows as follows:

For Small & Large:

Row 1: K2, *(P2, K2)* to end.

Row 2: P2, *(K2, P2)* to end.

For Medium: K2, P2 to end.

For all sizes: Change to #13 needle and work in St st. **At the same time,** increase 1 stitch at each edge every 8th row 7 (7, 9) times until you have 44 (46, 52) stitches. *Note: Increase leaving 2 edge stitches on either side of work. This means you should knit 2 stitches, increase a stitch, knit to the last 2 stitches, increase a stitch, and then knit the remaining 2 stitches. Increasing like this makes it easier to sew up your seams.* When sleeve measures 17″ (18″, 19.5″) from cast-on edge, ending with a WS row, SHAPE CAP: Bind off 3 stitches at the beginning of the next 2 rows. Bind off 2 stitches at the beginning of the following 2 rows. Then decrease 1 stitch at each edge every other row 3 (3, 5) times. Bind off 2 stitches at the beginning of the next 10 (10, 12) rows until 8 (8, 10) stitches remain. Bind off all stitches loosely.

FINISHING:

Sew shoulder seams together. Sew sleeves on. Sew down side and sleeve seams. (For more detailed instructions, see Finishing Techniques, page 29.)

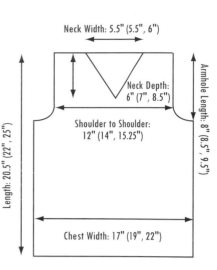

Neck Width: 5.5″ (5.5″, 6″)

Neck Depth: 6″ (7″, 8.5″)

Armhole Length: 8″ (8.5″, 9.5″)

Shoulder to Shoulder: 12″ (14″, 15.25″)

Length: 20.5″ (22″, 25″)

Chest Width: 17″ (19″, 22″)

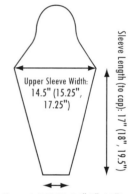

Upper Sleeve Width: 14.5″ (15.25″, 17.25″)

Sleeve Length (to cap): 17″ (18″, 19.5″)

Sleeve Cuff Width: 8.5″ (9″, 9.5″)

not your standard-issue sweatshirt, take two

In our first book, *The Yarn Girls' Guide to Simple Knits*, we included a hooded V-neck pullover with a seed-stitch border that continues to receive rave reviews. People just loved the idea of a knitted sweatshirt with a relaxed—but not slouchy—look. For this book, we added sophisticated features like cables and more seed-stitch detail. The three simple cables and seed-stitch panels are straightforward enough for first-time cablers—we promise! If you knit this, you're guaranteed to turn heads all winter long, whether you're sporting this hoodie around the block doing errands or having dinner with the in-laws.

> YARN: Blue Sky Alpaca, Worsted (100 yards / 100g ball)
> FIBER CONTENT: 50% Alpaca / 50% Merino Wool
> COLOR: 2007
> AMOUNT: 10 (11, 13) balls
> TOTAL YARDAGE: 1000 (1100, 1300) yards
> GAUGE: 3.5 stitches = 1 inch; 14 stitches = 4 inches
> NEEDLE SIZE: US 10 (6mm) or size needed to obtain gauge; US 8 (5mm) for ribbing; double-pointed or circular US 8 (5mm) to make I-cord
> SIZES: S (M, L)
> KNITTED MEASUREMENTS: Width = 18" (20", 22"); Length = 21.5" (23.5", 25"); Sleeve Length = 16.5" (17.5", 19")

PATTERN STITCH:

C6B = Place 3 stitches on a cable needle; hold at the back of the work. Knit 3 stitches from the left needle; knit 3 stitches from the cable needle.

BACK:

With #8 needle, cast on 70 (78, 86) stitches. Work in seed stitch for 8 rows as follows:

Row 1: *(K1, P1)* to end.

Row 2: *(P1, K1)* to end.

Change to #10 needle and work in pattern as follows:

Row 1: (K1, P1) 5 (6 , 7) times, K1, *P1, K6, P1, K12 (14, 16)*, repeat from * to *, P1, K6, P1, (P1, K1) 5 (6, 7) times, end P1.

Row 2: (P1, K 1) 5 (6, 7) times, P1 *K1, P6, K1, P12 (14, 16)*, repeat from * to *, K1, P6, K1, (P1, K1) 5 (6, 7) times, end K1.

Row 3: Work as for row 1.

Rows 4, 6, 8 & 10: Work as for row 2.

Row 5: (K1, P1) 5 (6, 7) times, K1, *P1, C6B, P1, K12 (14, 16)*, repeat from * to *, P1, C6B, P1, (P1, K1) 5 (6, 7) times, end P1.

Rows 7, 9 & 11: Work as for row 1.

Row 12: Work as for row 2.

Repeat this 12-row pattern until piece measures 13" (14.5", 15.5") from cast-on edge, ending with a WS row. SHAPE ARMHOLES: Bind off 3 stitches at the beginning of the next 2 rows. Bind off 2 stitches at the beginning of the following 2 rows. Then bind off 1 stitch at the beginning of the next 2 (6, 10) rows until 58 (62, 66) stitches remain. *(See step-by-step instructions on page 152.)* Continue working in pattern stitch until piece measures 21.5″ (23.5″, 25″) from cast-on edge, ending with a WS row. Bind off all stitches loosely.

FRONT:

Note: You may be shaping the armhole and the V-neck at the same time. Please read the instructions before proceeding.

Work as for back until piece measures 13″ (14.5″, 15.5″) from cast-on edge,-ending with a WS row. **SHAPE ARM-HOLES:** Bind off 3 stitches at the beginning of the next 2 rows. Bind off 2 stitches at the beginning of the following 2 rows. Then bind off 1 stitch at the beginning of the next 2 (6, 10) rows until 58 (62, 66) stitches remain. *(See step-by-step instructions on page 152.)* Continue working in pattern until piece measures 16.5″ (17.5″, 17.5″) from cast-on edge, ending with a WS row. Begin working center 24 (28, 32) stitches in seed stitch as follows:

Row 1: (K1, P1) 3 times, K6 (or C6B), P1, K4, (K1, P1) 12 (14, 16) times, K4, P1, K6 (or C6B), P1, (P1, K1) 2 times, end P1.

Row 2: (P1, K1) 3 times, P6, K1, P4, (P1, K1) 12 times, P4, K1, P6, K1, (K1, P1) 2 times, end K1.

Repeat rows 1 & 2 1 (2, 2) more time.

SHAPE V-NECK: Continue to work in pattern, keeping the center stitches in the established seed-stitch pattern. Place a marker at the center.

Row 1: Knit until 2 stitches before the marker, work 2tog in seed-stitch pattern. Turn work around as though you were at the end of the row. You are going to ignore the rest of the stitches.

Row 2: Work in pattern. Repeat rows 1 & 2 10 (11, 12) more times until 18 (19, 20) stitches remain. *(See step-by-step instructions on page 152.)* Continue to work on these stitches until piece measures 21.5″ (23.5″, 25″) from cast-on edge, ending with a WS row. Bind off all stitches loosely.

Attach yarn to other side. You should be on a RS row.

Row 1: Work 2tog in seed-stitch pattern. **Row 2:** Work in pattern. Repeat rows 1 & 2 10 (11, 12) more times until 18 (19, 20) stitches remain. *(See step-by-step instructions on page 152.)* Continue to work on these stitches until piece measures 21.5″ (23.5″, 25″) from cast-on edge, ending with a WS row. Bind off all stitches loosely.

SLEEVES:

With #8 needle, cast on 30 (34, 38) stitches. Work in seed stitch for 8 rows as follows:

Row 1: *(K1, P1)* to end.

Row 2: *(P1, K1)* to end.

Change to #10 needle and work in pattern stitch as follows:

Row 1: K11 (13, 15), P1, K6, P1, K11 (13, 15).

Rows 2, 4, 6, 8 & 10: P11 (13, 15), K1, P6, K1, P11 (13, 15).

Row 3: Work as for row 1.

Row 5: K11 (13, 15), P1, C6B, P1, K11 (13, 15).

Row 7 & 9: Work as for row 1.

Repeat rows 1 through 10 for sleeve pattern. **At the same time,** increase 1 stitch at each edge every 6th row 12 (12, 13) times until you have 54 (58, 64) stitches.

Note: Increase leaving 2 edge stitches on either side of work. This means you should knit 2 stitches, increase a stitch, knit to the last 2 stitches, increase a stitch, and then knit the remaining 2 stitches. Increasing like this makes it easier to sew up your seams.

When sleeve measures 16.5″ (17.5″, 19″) from cast-on edge, ending with a WS row, **SHAPE CAP:** Bind off 3 stitches at the beginning of the next 2 rows. Bind off 2 stitches at the beginning of the following 2 rows. Then bind off 1 stitch at the beginning of the next 2 (6, 10) rows. Bind off 2 stitches at the beginning of the next 16 (16, 18) rows until 10 (10, 8) stitches remain. Bind off all stitches loosely.

HOOD:

With #10 needle, cast on 41 stitches. Work first 21 stitches in seed stitch and remaining 22 stitches in St st as follows:
Row 1: (K1, P1) 10 times, knit to end.

Row 2: P22, (K1, P1) 10 times, end K1. Repeat rows 1 & 2 until hood measures 24″. Bind off all stitches loosely.

I-CORD:

Make a 3-stitch I-cord that is 50″ long (see page 37).

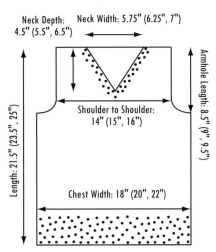

Neck Depth: 4.5" (5.5", 6.5")

Neck Width: 5.75" (6.25", 7")

Shoulder to Shoulder: 14" (15", 16")

Armhole Length: 8.5" (9", 9.5")

Length: 21.5" (23.5", 25")

Chest Width: 18" (20", 22")

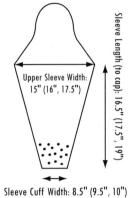

Upper Sleeve Width: 15" (16", 17.5")

Sleeve Length (to cap): 16.5" (17.5", 19")

Sleeve Cuff Width: 8.5" (9.5", 10")

FINISHING:

Sew shoulder seams together. Sew sleeves on. Sew down side and sleeve seams. (For more detailed instructions, see Finishing Techniques, page 29.)

Fold the hood in half and sew down the back side (the St st side). Then attach the hood to the body of the sweater by sewing it in around the back of the neck and about halfway down the V-neck. Fold the seed-stitch edge of the hood over the I-cord and sew it down.

Make 2 small tassels and attach them to each end of the I-cord.

cardigans

Cardigans are easy to get on and off for those days when it is hot one minute and cold the next. They can be used as a jacket in the fall or under a coat on a chilly day. Choosing the right buttons is always fun and is a way to further personalize the sweater, adding something special to an outfit. Give It a Whirl is a basic V-neck cardigan. It has a slim fit, and although the gauge is large, the yarn we used is actually quite light. It is the perfect sweater to throw on in a chilly restaurant or a frigid office or as an extra layer under your winter coat. Fabulously Funky has some straightforward decreases for a fun swing-coat effect. We used nubby yarn for a funky trim, but if you prefer, pick a plainer trim or use a smooth yarn. One Singular Sensation requires a simple and fun technique: knitting back and forth on a circular needle. There is one row of each color. It is a good way to incorporate colors to tie an outfit together. You can use subtle blending or use contrasting colors for some punch. The pattern for Slip and Slide calls for a cool stitch that produces a woven-like texture. We like it with a zipper (we had a tailor sew it in) but you can put in buttonholes if you wish. We used a chunky yarn so it knits up very quickly. Knit any sweater from this chapter and you'll be sitting pretty in no time.

give it a whirl

Michael, who is just twelve years old, was dead set on making a cardigan for his mother. We wrote a pattern for a V-neck with a garter-stitch border for him. He chose a bouclé-type yarn that helps hide flubs. He was very proud when he finished and told us matter-of-factly, "It was easy." So for all of you who have shied away from knitting sweaters, much less cardigans, listen to Michael and give it a whirl.

BACK:

With #10 needle, cast on 54 (58, 64) stitches. Work in garter stitch for 6 rows. Then work in St st until piece measures 11.5" (12.5", 14") from cast-on edge, ending with a WS row. S H A P E A R M H O L E S: Bind off 4 stitches at the beginning of the next 2 rows. Bind off 2 stitches at the beginning of the following 2 rows. Then decrease 1 stitch at each edge every other row 2 (2, 4) times until 38 (42, 44) stitches remain. *(See step-by-step instructions on page 153.)* Continue to work in St st until piece measures 19.5" (21", 23") from cast-on edge, ending with a WS row. Bind off all stitches loosely.

FRONT:
(make 2, reverse shaping)

Note: You may be shaping the armhole and the V-neck at the same time. Please read the instructions before proceeding.

With #10 needle, cast on 27 (29, 32) stitches. Work in garter stitch for 6 rows. Then work in St st until piece measures 11.5" (12.5", 14") from cast-on edge, ending with a WS row for the left front and a RS row for the right front. S H A P E A R M H O L E S A S F O R B A C K A T S I D E E D G E O N L Y until 19 (21, 22) stitches remain. *(See step-by-step instructions on page 153.)* Continue to work in St st until piece measures 13" (14", 15.5") from cast-on edge, ending with a RS row for the left front and a WS row for the right front. S H A P E V - N E C K: For left front when worn:

Row 1: Knit until last 4 stitches, K2tog, K2.

Rows 2 & 4: Purl.

Row 3: Knit.

Repeat rows 1 through 4 8 (9, 9) more times. *(See step-by-step instructions on page 153.)* Continue to work on remaining 10 (11, 12) stitches until piece measures 19.5" (21", 23") from cast-on edge, ending with a WS row. Bind off all stitches loosely.

For right front when worn:

Row 1: K2, SSK, knit to end.

Rows 2 & 4: Purl.

Row 3: Knit.

Repeat rows 1 through 4 8 (9, 9) more times. *(See step-by-step instructions on page 153.)* Continue to work on remaining 10 (11, 12) stitches until piece measures 19.5" (21", 23") from cast-on edge, ending with a WS row. Bind off all stitches loosely.

SLEEVES:

With #10 needle, cast on 28 (30, 32) stitches. Work in garter stitch for 6 rows. Then work in St st. **At the same time,** increase 1 stitch at each edge every 8th row 9 (9, 10) times until you have 46 (48, 52) stitches. *Note: Increase leaving 2 edge stitches on either side. This means you should knit 2 stitches, increase a stitch, knit to the last 2 stitches, increase a stitch, and then knit the remaining 2 stitches. Increasing like this makes it easier to sew up your seams.* When sleeve measures 17.5" (18.5", 19.5") from cast-on edge, ending with a WS row, S H A P E C A P: Bind off 4 stitches at the beginning of the next 2 rows. Bind off 2 stitches at the beginning of the following 2 rows. Then decrease 1 stitch at each edge every other row 1 (2, 4) time. Bind off 2 stitches at the beginning of the next 12 (10, 10) rows until 8 (12, 12) stitches remain. Bind off all stitches loosely.

FINISHING:

Sew shoulder seams together. Sew sleeves on. Sew up side and sleeve seams. (For more detailed instructions, see Finishing Techniques, page 29.) With the 32" circular #10 needle and RS facing, pick up 52 (56, 60) stitches up the right front to beginning of V-neck shaping, place marker (pm), pick up 26 (28, 30) stitches up right neck, pm, pick up 21 (23, 23) stitches across back neck, pm, pick up 26 (28, 30) down left neck to end of V-neck shaping, pm, pick up 52 (56, 60) stitches down left front. You will have 177 (191, 203) stitches. Knit 2 rows. Work buttonhole row: Work until second marker then K3 (YO, K2tog, K9 [10, 11]) 4 times, K2tog, YO, K3. Knit 3 rows. Bind off all stitches loosely.

YARN: GGH, Relax (115 yards / 50g ball)
FIBER CONTENT: 10% Alpaca / 32% Wool / 32% Polyamide / 26% Acrylic
COLOR: 37
AMOUNT: 5 (6, 7) balls
TOTAL YARDAGE: 575 (690, 805) yards
GAUGE: 3.25 stitches = 1 inch; 13 stitches = 4 inches
NEEDLE SIZE: US 10 (6mm) for body or size needed to obtain gauge; circular 32" US 10 (6mm) for neck and button-band ribbing
SIZES: S (M, L)
KNITTED MEASUREMENTS: Width = 17" (19", 21"); Length = 19.5" (21", 23"); Sleeve Length = 17.5" (18.5", 19.5")
OTHER MATERIALS: 5 buttons

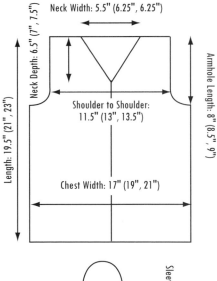

Neck Width: 5.5" (6.25", 6.25")
Neck Depth: 6.5" (7", 7.5")
Armhole Length: 8" (8.5", 9")
Length: 19.5" (21", 23")
Shoulder to Shoulder: 11.5" (13", 13.5")
Chest Width: 17" (19", 21")

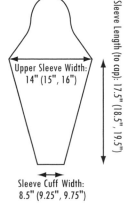

Upper Sleeve Width: 14" (15", 16")
Sleeve Length (to cap): 17.5" (18.5", 19.5")
Sleeve Cuff Width: 8.5" (9.25", 9.75")

fabulously funky

A few years ago we knit a cute baby coat with very bright colors as a sample for the store. Not only was it striped, but it had an A-line shape, bell sleeves, and a large collar. Cara, an avid knitter and a very frequent customer, came in and noticed our new addition right away. She loved it so much, she wanted to make it for herself. Not every adult woman could pull off wearing a striped coat like this one, but Cara could. She loved the coat and wore it quite a bit, but it was a little too loud to wear to work. So she made a toned-down version. She chose a solid color and knit the edgings and collars in a fun nubby yarn to give it a bit of funk. Now she has two, one for work and one for play.

BACK:

With #13 needle and yarn B, cast on 62 (68, 72) stitches. Work in garter stitch for 10 rows. Then change to 2 strands of yarn A and work 8 rows in St st. SHAPE A-LINE: Continue in St st, decreasing 1 stitch at each end of every 8th row, 9 (10, 10) times until 44 (48, 52) stitches remain. *(See step-by-step instructions on page 153.)* Continue in St st with no further decreasing until piece measures 26.5″ (28″, 29.5″) from cast-on edge, ending with a WS row. SHAPE ARMHOLES: Bind off 3 stitches at the beginning of the next 2 rows. Then decrease 1 stitch at each edge every other row 2 (3, 3) times until 34 (36, 40) stitches remain. *(See step-by-step instructions on page 153.)* Continue to work in St st until piece measures 35″ (37″, 39″) from cast-on edge, ending with a WS row. Bind off all stitches loosely.

FRONT:
(make 2, reverse shaping)

With #13 needle and yarn B, cast on 31 (34, 36) stitches. Work in garter stitch for 10 rows. Then change to 2 strands of yarn A and work in St st for 8 rows. SHAPE A-LINE: Continue in St st, decreasing 1 stitch at the outside edge every 8th row, 9 (10, 10) times, until 22 (24, 26) stitches remain. *(See step-by-step instructions on page 153.)* Continue in St st with no further decreasing until piece measures 26.5″ (28″, 29.5″) from cast-on edge, ending with a WS row for the left front and a RS row for the right front. SHAPE ARMHOLES AS FOR BACK AT SIDE EDGE ONLY (the same side that you did the decreases on) until 17 (18, 20) stitches remain. *(See step-by-step instructions on page 153.)* Continue to work in St st until piece measures 32.5″ (34.5″, 36.5″) from cast-on edge, ending with a RS row for the left front and a WS row for the right front. SHAPE CREW NECK: At the beginning of neck edge, every other row, bind off 3 stitches 1 time, 2

stitches 1 time, 1 stitch 2 (2, 3) times. *(See step-by-step instructions on page 153.)* Continue to work on remaining 10 (11, 12) stitches until piece measures 35″ (37″, 39″) from cast-on edge, ending with a WS row. Bind off all stitches loosely.

SLEEVES:

With #13 needle and yarn B, cast on 30 (32, 34) stitches. Work in garter stitch for 10 rows. Change to 2 strands of yarn A and work in St st; **at the same time** decrease 1 stitch at each edge every other row 4 (4, 5) times until 22 (24, 24) stitches remain. Continue working in St st and, **at the same time,** increase 1 stitch at each edge every 6th row 7 (8, 9) times until you have 36 (40, 42) stitches. *Note: Increase leaving 2 edge stitches on either side. This means you should knit 2 stitches, increase a stitch, knit to the last 2 stitches, increase a stitch, and then knit the remaining 2 stitches. Increasing like this makes it easier to sew up your seams.* When sleeve measures 18″ (19″, 20.5″) from cast-on edge, ending with a WS row, SHAPE CAP: Bind off 3 stitches at the beginning of the next 2 rows. Then decrease 1 stitch at each edge every other row 2 (3, 3) times. Bind off 2 stitches at the beginning of the next 8 (8, 10) rows until 10 (10, 12) stitches remain. Bind off all stitches loosely.

FINISHING:

Sew shoulder seams together. Sew sleeves on. Sew up side and sleeve seams. (For more detailed instructions, see Finishing Techniques, page 29.)

With #13 needle, yarn B, and the WS facing you, pick up 38 (40, 40) stitches around neck edge. Work in garter stitch for 4.5″. Bind off all stitches loosely.

With #13 needle, yarn B, and the RS facing you, pick up 90 (96, 102) stitches up side edge. Bind off all stitches loosely.

YARNS: A: Crystal Palace Yarns, Merino Frappe (140 yards / 50g ball); B: Gedifra, Sheela (33 yards / 50g ball)
FIBER CONTENT: A: 80% Merino Wool / 20% Polyamide; B: 48% New Wool / 48% Acrylic / 4% Polyamide
COLORS: A: 24; B: 4112
AMOUNT: A: 8 (10, 12) balls; B: 4 (5, 6) balls
TOTAL YARDAGE: A: 1120 (1400, 1680) yards; B: 132 (165, 198) yards
GAUGE: 2.5 stitches = 1 inch; 10 stitches = 4 inches
NEEDLE SIZE: US 13 (9mm) or size needed to obtain gauge
SIZES: S (M, L)
KNITTED MEASUREMENTS: Bottom Width = 25″ (27″, 29″); Chest Width = 17.5″ (19″, 21″); Length = 35″ (37″, 39″); Sleeve Length = 18″ (19″, 20.5″)
Yarn A is worked double throughout the sweater—this means you should hold 2 strands of A together as though they are 1.

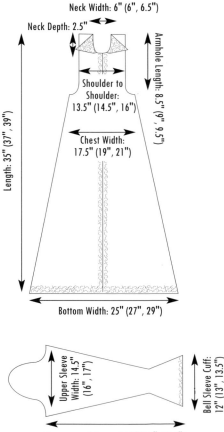

Neck Width: 6″ (6″, 6.5″)
Neck Depth: 2.5″
Armhole Length: 8.5″ (9″, 9.5″)
Shoulder to Shoulder: 13.5″ (14.5″, 16″)
Chest Width: 17.5″ (19″, 21″)
Length: 35″ (37″, 39″)
Bottom Width: 25″ (27″, 29″)

Upper Sleeve Width: 14.5″ (16″, 17″)
Bell Sleeve Cuff: 12″ (13″, 13.5″)
Sleeve Length (to cap): 18″ (19″, 20.5″)

one singular sensation

Rachel wanted to knit a sweater with "skinny stripes." She wanted a multicolor affair that would go with everything in her closet. She thought that thick stripes, even a two-row stripe pattern, was too casual for her office. So we picked a few colors of yarn and taught her how to knit a single-stripe pattern, which is a lot of fun. To make single stripes, you slide the yarn and knit from either end while using a pair of circular needles. This method is great because it cuts down on the number of ends that need to be woven in.

YARN: Debbie Bliss, Cashmerino Aran (95 yards / 50g ball)
FIBER CONTENT: 55% Merino Wool / 33% Microfibre / 12% Cashmere
COLORS: A: 300102; B: 300207; C: 300103; D: 300105; E: 300617
AMOUNT: 2 (3, 3) balls of each color
TOTAL YARDAGE: 950 (1425, 1425) yards
GAUGE: 4 stitches = 1 inch; 16 stitches = 4 inches
NEEDLE SIZE: US 10 (6mm) for body or size needed to obtain gauge; US 9 (5.5mm) for ribbing
SIZES: S (M, L)
KNITTED MEASUREMENTS: Width = 17" (19", 21"); Length = 19.5" (20.5", 23"); Sleeve Length = 17.5" (18.5", 19.5")
OTHER MATERIALS: 5 buttons

STRIPE PATTERN:

1-row stripe as follows:

Row 1: A.

Row 2: B.

Row 3: A.

Row 4: D.

Row 5: C.

Row 6: E.

Row 7: C.

Row 8: D.

Row 9: B.

Row 10: A.

Row 11: B.

Row 12: D.

Row 13: E.

Row 14: C.

Row 15: E.

Row 16: D.

Repeat rows 1 through 16.

BACK:

With #9 needle and color D, cast on 68 (76, 84) stitches. Work in seed stitch for 6 rows as follows:

Row 1: *K1, P1* to end.

Row 2: *P1, K1* to end.

Change to #10 needle and work in St st and stripe pattern until piece measures 11.5" (12", 14") from cast-on edge, ending with a WS row. SHAPE ARMHOLES: Bind off 4 stitches at the beginning of the next 0 (2, 2) rows. Bind off 3 stitches at the beginning of the next 2 rows. Bind off 2 stitches at the beginning of the next 2 rows. Then decrease 1 stitch at each edge, every other row 3 (1, 3) times until 52 (56, 60) stitches remain. *(See step-by-step instructions on page 154.)* Continue to work in St st until piece measures 19.5" (20.5", 23") from cast-on edge, ending with a WS row. Bind off all stitches loosely.

FRONT:
(make 2, reverse shaping)

With #9 needle and color D, cast on 34 (38, 42) stitches. Work in seed stitch for 6 rows as follows:

Row 1: *K1, P1* to end.

Row 2: *P1, K1* to end.

Change to #10 needle and work in St st and stripe pattern until piece measures 11.5" (12", 14") from cast-on edge, ending with a WS row for the left front and a RS row for the right front.

SHAPE ARMHOLES AS FOR BACK AT SIDE EDGE ONLY until 26 (28, 30) stitches remain. *(See step-by-step instructions on page 154.)* Continue to work in St st until piece measures 17" (18", 20") from cast-on edge, ending with a WS row for the right front and a RS row for the left front. SHAPE CREW NECK: At the beginning of each neck edge, every other row, bind off 5 stitches once, 3 stitches once, 2 stitches once, 1 stitch 2 (3, 4) times. *(See step-by-step instructions on page 154.)* Continue to work on remaining 14 (15, 16) stitches until piece measures 19.5" (20.5", 23") from cast-on edge, ending with a WS row. Bind off all stitches loosely.

SLEEVES:

With #9 needle and color D, cast on 32 (36, 40) stitches. Work in seed stitch for 6 rows as follows:

Row 1: *K1, P1* to end.

Row 2: *P1, K1* to end.

Change to #10 needle and work in St st and stripe pattern. **At the same time,** increase 1 stitch at each edge every 6th row 13 (13, 12) times, until you have 58 (62, 64) stitches. *Note: Increase leaving 2 edge stitches on either side. This means you should knit 2 stitches, increase a stitch, knit to the last 2 stitches, increase a stitch, and then knit the remaining 2 stitches. Increasing like this makes it easier to sew up your seams.*

When sleeve measures 17.5" (18.5", 19.5") from cast-on edge, ending with a WS row, SHAPE CAP: Bind off 4 stitches at the beginning of the next 0 (2, 2) rows. Bind off 3 stitches at the beginning of the next 2 rows. Bind off 2 stitches at the beginning of the next 2 rows. Then decrease 1 stitch at each edge every other row 3 (1, 3) times. Bind off 2 stitches at the beginning of the next 14 (14, 12) rows until 14 (14, 16) stitches remain. Bind off all stitches loosely.

FINISHING:

Sew shoulder seams together. Sew sleeves on. Sew up side and sleeve seams. With #9 needle, color D, and RS of right front neck facing you, pick up 59 (61, 63) stitches around the neck. (For more detailed instructions, see Finishing Techniques, page 29.) Work in seed stitch for 5 rows. Bind off all stitches loosely in seed stitch. BUTTON BAND: With #9 needle, color D, and RS facing you, pick up 75 (79, 85) stitches. Work in seed stitch for 5 rows.

Bind off all stitches loosely in seed stitch. BUTTONHOLE BAND: With #9 needle, color D, and RS facing you, pick up 75 (79, 85) stitches. Work in seed stitch for 2 rows. Make buttonholes as follows: Seed 3 (3, 4) stitches, *YO, seed 2 together, seed 15 (16, 17) stitches*, repeat from * to * 3 more times, end YO, seed 2 together, seed 2 (2, 3). Work in seed stitch for 2 more rows. Bind off all stitches loosely in seed stitch.

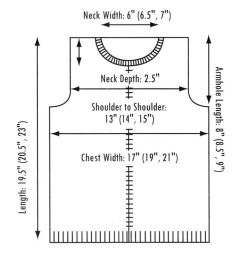

Neck Width: 6" (6.5", 7")

Neck Depth: 2.5"

Shoulder to Shoulder: 13" (14", 15")

Chest Width: 17" (19", 21")

Armhole Length: 8" (8.5", 9")

Length: 19.5" (20.5", 23")

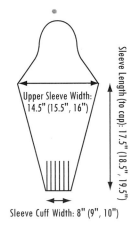

Upper Sleeve Width: 14.5" (15.5", 16")

Sleeve Length (to cap): 17.5" (18.5", 19.5")

Sleeve Cuff Width: 8" (9", 10")

slip and slide

We saw Evelyn all the time because she would knit a new sweater each week, until all of a sudden she disappeared. As it turns out, Evelyn had too many sweaters and not enough closet space. Yet, as soon as she saw Julie wearing this sweater, she fell in love with its woven texture, had to get the yarn, learn the slip stitch pattern, and make her "last sweater." She got hooked on knitting all over again, and she once more comes in every week —but now she makes gifts.

PATTERN STITCH:
(worked on even number of stitches)

Row 1: K1, *K1, sl 1 purlwise (pw) with yarn in front (wyif); repeat from * to last stitch, end K1.

Rows 2 & 4: Purl.

Row 3: K1, *sl 1 pw wyif, K1; repeat from * to last stitch, end K1.

BACK:

With #15 needle, cast on 36 (40, 44) stitches. Work in K1, P1 ribbing for 6 rows. Change to #17 needle and begin to work in pattern stitch until piece measures 12″ (13.5″, 14″) from cast-on edge, ending with a WS row. SHAPE ARMHOLES: Bind off 3 stitches at the beginning of the next 0 (2, 2) rows. Bind off 2 stitches at the beginning of the next 2 rows. Then decrease 1 stitch at each edge every other row 3 (1, 2) times until 26 (28, 30) stitches remain. *(See step-by-step instructions on page 154.)* Continue to work in St st until piece measures 21″ (23″, 24″) from cast-on edge, ending with a WS row. Bind off all stitches loosely.

FRONT:
(make 2, reverse shaping)

With #15 needle, cast on 18 (20, 22) stitches. Work in K1, P1 ribbing for 6 rows. Change to #17 needle and begin to work in pattern stitch until piece measures 12″ (13.5″, 14″) from cast-on edge, ending with a WS row for the left front and a RS row for the right front. SHAPE ARMHOLES AS FOR BACK AT SIDE EDGE ONLY until 13 (14, 15) stitches remain. *(See step-by-step instructions on page 154.)* Continue to work in pattern stitch until piece measures 18.5″ (20.5″, 21″) from cast-on edge, ending with a WS row for the right front and a RS row for the left front. SHAPE CREW NECK: At the beginning of each neck edge, every other row, bind off 3 stitches once, 2 stitches once, 1 stitch

1 (2, 2) times. *(See step-by-step instructions on page 154.)* Continue to work on remaining 7 (7, 8) stitches until piece measures 21″ (23″, 24″) from cast-on edge, ending with a WS row. Bind off all stitches loosely.

SLEEVES:

With #15 needle, cast on 16 (18, 20) stitches. Work in K1, P1 ribbing for 6 rows. Change to #17 needle and work in pattern stitch. **At the same time,** increase 1 stitch at each edge every 8th row 6 times until you have 28 (30, 32) stitches. *Note: Increase leaving 2 edge stitches on either side. This means you should knit 2 stitches, increase a stitch, knit to the last 2 stitches, increase a stitch, and then knit the remaining 2 stitches. Increasing like this makes it easier to sew up your seams.* When sleeve measures 17.5″ (18.5″, 19.5″) from cast-on edge, ending with a WS row, SHAPE CAP: Bind off 3 stitches at the beginning of the next 0 (2, 2) rows. Bind off 2 stitches at the beginning of the next 2 rows. Then decrease 1 stitch at each edge every other row 3 (1, 2) times. Bind off 2 stitches at the beginning of the next 6 rows until 6 stitches remain. Bind off all stitches loosely.

FINISHING:

Sew shoulder seams together. Sew sleeves on. Sew up side and sleeve seams. (For more detailed instructions, see Finishing Techniques, page 29.) With #15 needle and RS facing you, pick up 26 (28, 28) stitches around the neck. Work in K1, P1 ribbing for 4 rows. Bind off all stitches loosely. With #15 needle and RS facing you, pick up 50 (54, 58) stitches up side band and work in K1, P1 ribbing for 3 rows. Bind off all stitches loosely. Repeat this for the band on the other side. Take to the tailor and ask the person behind the counter to sew in an appropriately sized zipper.

YARN: Blue Sky Alpaca, Blue Sky Bulky (45 yards / 100g ball)
FIBER CONTENT: 50% Alpaca / 50% Wool
COLOR: 1007
AMOUNT: 10 (12, 14) balls
TOTAL YARDAGE: 450 (540, 630) yards
GAUGE: 2 stitches = 1 inch; 8 stitches = 4 inches
NEEDLE SIZE: US 17 (12mm) or size needed to obtain gauge; US 15 (10mm) for ribbing
SIZES: S (M, L)
KNITTED MEASUREMENTS: Width = 18″ (20″, 22″); Length = 21″ (23″, 24″); Sleeve Length = 17.5″ (18.5″, 19.5″)
OTHER MATERIALS: A zipper

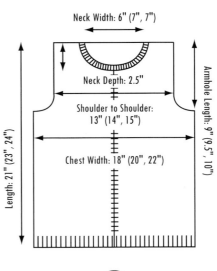

Neck Width: 6″ (7″, 7″)
Neck Depth: 2.5″
Shoulder to Shoulder: 13″ (14″, 15″)
Armhole Length: 9″ (9.5″, 10″)
Length: 21″ (23″, 24″)
Chest Width: 18″ (20″, 22″)

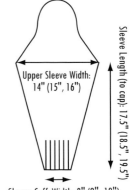

Upper Sleeve Width: 14″ (15″, 16″)
Sleeve Length (to cap): 17.5″ (18.5″, 19.5″)
Sleeve Cuff Width: 8″ (9″, 10″)

tees and tanks

We have included six projects for your spring and summer wardrobe —three tanks and three T-shirts. We knit them in lightweight fibers such as cotton, rayon, and viscose. However, you can knit them in whatever you want—wool, alpaca, cashmere, or any other fiber—as long as you get the proper gauge. A Table for Two is knit in stockinette stitch and has a crocheted border around all of its edges. We used a cotton/nylon blend that has a little shimmer and a lot of drape. The Mysterious Case of the Missing Tee has a square neckline that is mitered at the corners. It is knit in a 6-row stripe pattern, using three colors. You can make it in one color, two colors, or ten colors—the choice is yours; you can just use our pattern as the basic outline and go from there. A Sweater for the Ages has a polo neck, which is shaped more like the neck of a cardigan than a pullover. Tank You Very Much is a basic tank top with a rolled edge at the bottom and a crocheted border. It is a great shape to wear with a flowy summer skirt or under a jacket at work, and it's also perfect with jeans. The Same . . . but Different has a simple lace stitch used at the bottom and a few inches under the bust line. Tara's Tank is a good first cable project, even though the cable we chose is a little more challenging than a basic cable. You'll need to use the cable needle every other row, but it's worth the extra bit of work because the end product comes out beautifully. The variety in this chapter will keep you in stitches all year long!

a table for two

Jordana and Julie went downtown to one of New York City's trendy restaurants. When they walked in they noticed the hostess, Nici, wearing a knit T-shirt. Jordana requested a table for two and asked Nici where she got the T-shirt. Nici laughed and said, "I got it from you guys." She said she'd been wearing the top at the restaurant and had gotten tons of compliments. Then she asked, "By the way, do you need any help at the store?" We did, and that was the beginning of a beautiful relationship.

BACK:

With #9 needle, cast on 64 (72, 80) stitches. Work in St st until piece measures 12" (14", 15.5") from the cast-on edge, ending with a WS row. SHAPE ARMHOLES: Bind off 4 stitches at the beginning of the next 2 rows 0 (0, 1) times. Bind off 3 stitches at the beginning of the next 2 rows. Bind off 2 stitches at the beginning of the following 2 rows. Then decrease 1 stitch at each edge every other row 1 (4, 3) time until 52 (54, 56) stitches remain. *(See step-by-step instructions on page 155.)* Continue working in St st until piece measures 19" (21.5", 23.5") from cast-on edge, ending with a WS row. Bind off all stitches loosely.

FRONT:

Work as for back until piece measures 12" (14", 15.5") from cast-on edge, ending with a WS row. SHAPE ARMHOLES: Bind off 4 stitches at the beginning of the next 2 rows 0 (0, 1) times. Bind off 3 stitches at the beginning of the next 2 rows. Bind off 2 stitches at the beginning of the following 2 rows. Then decrease 1 stitch at each edge every other row 1 (4, 3) time until 52 (54, 56) stitches remain. *(See step-by-step instructions on page 155.)* Continue working in St st until piece measures 16.5" (19", 21") from cast-on edge, ending with a WS row.

SHAPE CREW NECK: Bind off center 14 (16, 16) stitches. Working each side of neck separately, at the beginning of each neck edge, every other row, bind off 3 stitches 1 time, 2 stitches 1 time, 1 stitch 1 time. *(See step-by-step instructions on page 155.)* Continue to work on the remaining 13 (13, 14) stitches with no further decreasing until piece measures 19" (21.5", 23.5") from cast-on edge, ending with a WS row. Bind off all stitches loosely.

SLEEVES:

With #9 needle cast on 44 (50, 56) stitches. Work in St st. **At the same time,** increase 1 stitch at each edge every other row 3 times until you have 50 (56, 62) stitches. *Note: Increase leaving 2 edge stitches on either side. This means you should knit 2 stitches, increase a stitch, knit to the last 2 stitches, increase a stitch, and then knit the remaining 2 stitches. Increasing like this makes it easier to sew up your seams.* When sleeve measures 2.5" (3.5", 4") from cast-on edge, ending with a WS row, SHAPE CAP: Bind off 4 stitches at the beginning of the next 2 rows 0 (0, 1) times. Bind off 3 stitches at the beginning of the next 2 rows. Bind off 2 stitches at the beginning of the following 2 rows. Then

decrease 1 stitch at each edge every other row 1 (4, 3) time. Bind off 2 stitches at the beginning of the next 14 rows until 10 stitches remain. Bind off all stitches loosely.

FINISHING:

Sew shoulder seams together. Sew sleeves on. Sew up side and sleeve seams. (For more detailed instructions, see Finishing Techniques, page 29.) With an H crochet hook, work 1 row single crochet, then 1 row shrimp stitch around bottom, sleeve, and neck edges.

YARN: Knit One, Crochet Too, Tartelette (75 yards / 50g ball)
FIBER CONTENT: 50% Cotton / 40% Tactel Nylon / 10% Nylon
COLOR: 618
AMOUNT: 6 (8, 10) balls
TOTAL YARDAGE: 450 (600, 750) yards
GAUGE: 4 stitches = 1 inch;
16 stitches = 4 inches
NEEDLE SIZE: US 9 (5.5mm) or size needed to obtain gauge; H crochet hook
SIZES: S (M, L)
KNITTED MEASUREMENTS: Width = 16" (18", 20"); Length = 19" (21.5", 23.5"); Sleeve Length = 2.5" (3.5", 4")

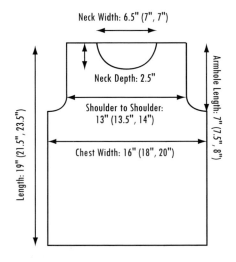

Neck Width: 6.5" (7", 7")
Neck Depth: 2.5"
Shoulder to Shoulder: 13" (13.5", 14")
Armhole Length: 7" (7.5", 8")
Chest Width: 16" (18", 20")
Length: 19" (21.5", 23.5")

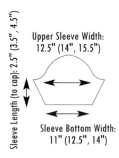

Sleeve Length (to cap): 2.5" (3.5", 4.5")
Upper Sleeve Width: 12.5" (14", 15.5")
Sleeve Bottom Width: 11" (12.5", 14")

the mysterious case
of the missing tee

Every once in a while, we noticed that a cute knit tank or tee would disappear for a day or two from our store and then miraculously reappear like it had never been gone in the first place. One afternoon we were discussing this freaky phenomenon when Ellen, a customer of ours, turned beet red. "I'm so mortified," she said. "I am the culprit." She explained that she was making a tank top that we had also had as a sample and accidentally scooped it up along with the stuff she was working on when she left. She brought it back two days later when she noticed. Another time she had tried on a T-shirt and forgotten to take it off, "just like the last time," she said, sheepishly pulling out this very striped sweater with a square neck from her bag. "Your things just fit me so perfectly that I forget they aren't mine. And I put them back without saying anything because I was so embarrassed." We all laughed, happy that the mystery was solved.

YARN: Online, Clip
(166 yards / 100g ball)
FIBER CONTENT: 100% Cotton
COLORS: A: 157; B: 171; C: 05
AMOUNT: A: 2 (2, 3) balls; B: 2 (2, 3) balls; C: 2 (2, 3) balls
TOTAL YARDAGE: 996 (996, 1494) yards
GAUGE: 5 stitches = 1 inch; 20 stitches = 4 inches
NEEDLE SIZE: US 7 (4.5mm) for body or size needed to obtain gauge; US 5 (3.75mm) for ribbing; circular 16" US 5 (3.75mm) for picking up stitches around neck
SIZES: S (M, L)
KNITTED MEASUREMENTS: Width = 16" (18", 20"); Length = 19.5" (21.5", 23.5"); Sleeve Length = 2.5" (3.5", 4.5")

STRIPE PATTERN:

6 rows St st in color A

6 rows St st in color B

6 rows St st in color C

BACK:

With #5 needle and color A, cast on 80 (90, 100) stitches. Work in K1, P1 ribbing for 6 rows. Change to #7 needle and work in St st stripe pattern, beginning with color B, until piece measures 12″ (13.5″, 14.5″) from cast-on edge, ending with a WS row. SHAPE ARMHOLES: Bind off 4 stitches at the beginning of the next 0 (0, 2) rows. Bind off 3 stitches at the beginning of the next 2 rows. Bind off 2 stitches at the beginning of the following 2 rows. Then decrease 1 stitch at each edge every other row 4 (6, 6) times until 62 (68, 70) stitches remain. *(See step-by-step instructions on page 155.)* Continue working in St st until piece measures 19.5″ (21.5″, 23.5″) from cast-on edge, ending with a WS row. Bind off all stitches loosely.

FRONT:

Work as for back until piece measures 12″ (13.5″, 14.5″) from cast-on edge, ending with a WS row. SHAPE ARMHOLES: Bind off 4 stitches at the beginning of the next 0 (0, 2) rows. Bind off 3 stitches at the beginning of the next 2 rows. Bind off 2 stitches at the beginning of the following 2 rows. Then decrease 1 stitch at each edge every other row 4 (6, 6) times until 62 (68, 70) stitches remain. *(See step-by-step instructions on page 155.)* Continue working in St st until piece measures 16″ (18″, 19.5″) from cast-on edge, ending with a WS row. SHAPE NECK: Bind off center 32 (36, 38) stitches. Begin working each side of the neck separately, working on 15 (16, 17) stitches until piece measures 19.5″ (21.5″, 23.5″) from cast-on edge, ending with a WS row. *(See step-by-step instructions on page 155.)* Bind off all stitches loosely.

SLEEVES:

With #5 needle and color A, cast on 56 (62, 70) stitches. Work in K1, P1 ribbing for 6 rows. Change to #7 needle and work in St st stripe pattern, beginning with color B. **At the same time,** increase 1 stitch at each edge every other row 2 (3, 5) times until you have 60 (68, 80) stitches. *Note: Increase leaving 2 edge stitches on either side. This means you should knit 2 stitches, increase a stitch, knit to the last 2 stitches, increase a stitch, and then knit the remaining 2 stitches. Increasing like this makes it easier to sew up your seams.* When sleeve measures 2.5″ (3.5″, 4.5″) from cast-on edge, ending with a WS row, SHAPE CAP: Bind off 4 stitches at the beginning of the next 0 (0, 2) rows. Bind off 3 stitches at the beginning of the next 2 rows. Bind off 2 stitches at the beginning of the following 2 rows. Then decrease 1 stitch at each edge every other row 4 (6, 6) times. Bind off 2 stitches at the beginning of the next 18 (20, 22) rows until 6 stitches remain. Bind off all stitches loosely.

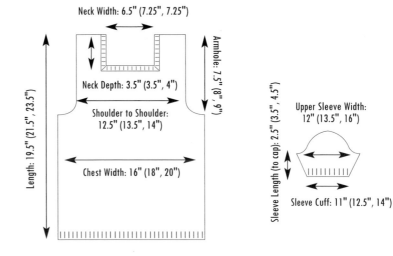

Neck Width: 6.5" (7.25", 7.25")

Neck Depth: 3.5" (3.5", 4")

Armhole: 7.5" (8", 9")

Shoulder to Shoulder: 12.5" (13.5", 14")

Length: 19.5" (21.5", 23.5")

Chest Width: 16" (18", 20")

Sleeve Length (to cap): 2.5" (3.5", 4.5")

Upper Sleeve Width: 12" (13.5", 16")

Sleeve Cuff: 11" (12.5", 14")

FINISHING:

Sew shoulder seams together. Sew sleeves on. Sew up side and sleeve seams. Pick up stitches for neck as follows: With a 16″ circular #5 needle and color A, pick up 32 (36, 38) stitches from the back neck, place a marker (pm), pick up 27 (27, 29) stitches down the left neck, pm, pick up 32 (36, 38) stitches from the front neck, pm, pick up 27 (27, 29) stitches from the right neck, pm. (For more detailed instructions, see Finishing Techniques, page 29.) Work in K1, P1 ribbing for 6 rows, decreasing 1 stitch before and after each marker on each round. Bind off all stitches loosely.

Note: Decreases before markers should be K2tog. Decreases after markers should be SSK.

a sweater for the ages

Linore came in one day looking for a sweater to make with buttons she'd taken off an old sweater her mother had made—but she only had three left. The buttons had a summery look about them so we thought a tank top knit in a lightweight yarn with a placket (a neckline similar to ones found on polo shirts) would solve the problem. But Linore took Julie aside and told her, "Honey, no tank tops. Look at my upper arm; you know I'm of a certain age." Julie thought her arms looked just fine, but she wasn't going to argue with a customer, so she suggested that Linore make a long-sleeve sweater with a placket. "No way," Linore said. "I get very hot, especially in the summer; you know I'm of a certain age." So Julie designed a pattern for a cap-sleeve T-shirt, which would cover Linore's upper arms and leave her feeling cool at the same time. We loved it so much we made the same one. We discovered cap sleeves accentuate nicely toned arms as well as cover up those that aren't.

YARN: Artful Yarns, Fable
(184 yards / 50g ball)
FIBER CONTENT: 85% Pima Cotton /
15% Silk
COLOR: 95
AMOUNT: 3 (4, 5) balls
TOTAL YARDAGE: 552 (736, 920) yards
GAUGE: 4.25 stitches = 1 inch;
17 stitches = 4 inches
NEEDLE SIZE: US 8 (5mm) or size
needed to obtain gauge; US 6 (4mm)
for ribbing
SIZES: S (M, L)
KNITTED MEASUREMENTS: Width = 16″
(17.5″, 19″); Length = 19″ (20.5″, 22″)
OTHER MATERIALS: 3 buttons

BACK:

With #6 needle, cast on 68 (74, 82) stitches. Work in K2, P2 ribbing for 10 rows as follows:

For Small: K2, P2.

For Medium & Large:

Row 1: K2 *P2, K2* to end.

Row 2: P2 *K2, P2* to end.

For all sizes: Change to #8 needle and work in St st until piece measures 12" (12.5", 13.5") from cast-on edge, ending with a WS row. SHAPE ARMHOLES: Bind off 4 stitches at the beginning of the next 2 rows 0 (0, 1) times. Bind off 3 stitches at the beginning of the next 2 rows. Bind off 2 stitches at the beginning of the next 2 rows. Then decrease 1 stitch at each edge every other row 3 (3, 2) times until 52 (58, 60) stitches remain. *(See step-by-step instructions on page 155.)* Continue to work in St st until piece measures 19" (20.5", 22") from cast-on edge, ending with a WS row. Bind off remaining stitches loosely.

FRONT:

Work as for back until piece measures 12" (12.5", 13.5") from cast-on edge, ending with a WS row. SHAPE ARMHOLES: Bind off 4 stitches at the beginning of the next 2 rows 0 (0, 1) times. Bind off 3 stitches at the beginning of the following 2 rows. Bind off 2 stitches at the beginning of the next 2 rows. Then decrease 1 stitch at each edge every other row 3 (3, 2) times until 52 (58, 60) stitches remain. *(See step-by-step instructions on page 155.)* Continue in St st until piece measures 14" (15", 16") from cast-on edge, ending with a WS row.

Bind off center 4 stitches. Working each side separately, continue in St st on remaining 24 (27, 28) stitches until piece measures 16.5" (18", 19.5") from cast-on edge, ending with a RS row for the left front and a WS row for the right front. SHAPE NECK: At the beginning of each neck edge, every other row, bind off 4 stitches 1 time, 3 stitches 1 time, 2 stitches 1 time, 1 stitch 3 (3, 4) times. *(See step-by-step instructions on page 156.)* Continue to work in St st with no further shaping on remaining 12 (15, 15) stitches until piece measures 19" (20.5", 22") from cast-on edge, ending with a WS row. Bind off all stitches loosely.

SLEEVES:

With #6 needle, cast on 48 (52, 58) stitches. Work in K2, P2 ribbing for 6 rows as follows:

For Small & Medium: K2, P2 every row.

For Large:

Row 1: K2 *P2, K2* to end.

Row 2: P2 *K2, P2* to end.

For all sizes: Change to #8 needle and work in St st for 2 (6, 8) rows. SHAPE CAP: Bind off 4 stitches at the beginning of the next 2 rows 0 (0, 1) times. Bind off 3 stitches at the beginning of the next 2 rows. Bind off 2 stitches at the beginning of the next 2 rows. Then decrease 1 stitch at each end every other row 3 (3, 2) times. Bind off 2 stitches at the beginning of the next 14 (16, 16) rows until 14 stitches remain. Bind off all stitches loosely.

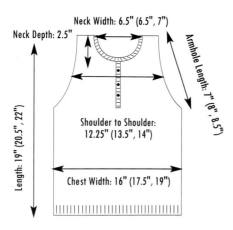

Neck Depth: 2.5"

Neck Width: 6.5" (6.5", 7")

Armhole Length: 7" (8", 8.5")

Length: 19" (20.5", 22")

Shoulder to Shoulder: 12.25" (13.5", 14")

Chest Width: 16" (17.5", 19")

Sleeve Cuff Width: 11" (12.25", 13.5")

FINISHING:

Sew shoulder seams together. Sew sleeves on. Sew up side and sleeve seams. (For more detailed instructions, see Finishing Techniques, page 29.)

NECKBAND: With #6 needle and RS facing you, pick up 58 (58, 62) stitches around neck. Work in K2, P2 ribbing for 6 rows as follows:

Row 1: K2 *P2, K2* to end.

Row 2: P2 *K2, P2* to end.

Bind off loosely.

Note: Buttonholes should be placed on the right front as the sweater is worn.

BUTTONHOLE BAND: With #6 needle and RS facing, pick up 16 (18, 22) stitches. Work in K2, P2 ribbing for 2 rows as follows:

For Small: K2, P2 every row.

For Medium & Large:

Row 1: K2 *P2, K2* to end.

Row 2: P2 *K2, P2* to end.

Buttonholes: Rib 2 (3, 2), (YO, rib 2 tog, rib 3 [3, 6]) 2 times, end rib 2tog, YO, rib 2 (3, 2). Work 2 more rows in K2, P2 ribbing. Bind off all stitches loosely.

BUTTON BAND: With #6 needle and RS facing you, pick up 16 (18, 22) stitches. Work 5 rows in K2, P2 rib as follows:

For Small: K2, P2 every row.

For Medium & Large:

Row 1: K2 *P2, K2* to end.

Row 2: P2 *K2, P2* to end.

Bind off all stitches loosely.

tank you
very much

Julie, her husband, John, and their one-and-a-half-year-old daughter, Olivia, had plans to visit her parents at their beach house. Julie was dead set on finishing her knitting project before the weekend was over. She knitted this tank top every chance she got, in all the likely places and during every free moment—in the car during the drive there, at the beach house during Olivia's naps, even on the beach. When she was done, Julie modeled the finished product for her parents. After Julie's mom told her that she loved it, Julie said, "Thank you." Julie's father, a known cornball, piped up and said, "No, you mean, 'tank you.'"

BACK:

With #7 needle and color A, cast on 80 (90, 100) stitches. Work in St st until piece measures 12″ (13.5″, 15″) from cast-on edge. SHAPE ARMHOLES: Bind off 4 stitches at the beginning of the next 2 rows. Bind off 3 stitches at the beginning of the following 2 rows. Bind off 2 stitches at the beginning of the next 2 rows. Then decrease 1 stitch at each edge every other row 1 (3, 6) times until 60 (66, 70) stitches remain. *(See step-by-step instructions on page 156.)* Continue working in St st until piece measures 19″ (21″, 23″) from cast-on edge, ending with a WS row. Bind off all stitches loosely.

FRONT:

Work as for back until piece measures 12″ (13.5″, 15″) from cast-on edge, ending with a WS row. SHAPE ARMHOLES: Bind off 4 stitches at the beginning of the next 2 rows. Bind off 3 stitches at the beginning of the following 2 rows. Bind off 2 stitches at the beginning of the next 2 rows. Then decrease 1 stitch at each edge every other row 1 (3, 6) times until 60 (66, 70) stitches remain. *(See step-by-step instructions on page 156.)* Continue working in St st until piece measures 16.5″ (18.5″, 20.5″) from cast-on edge, ending with a WS row. SHAPE CREW NECK: Bind off center 20 (22, 24) stitches and then begin working each side of the neck separately. At the beginning of each neck edge, every other row, bind off 3 stitches 1 time, 2 stitches 1 time, 1 stitch 2 times. *(See step-by-step instructions on page 156.)* Continue to work on remaining 13 (15, 16) stitches with no further decreasing until piece measures 19″ (21″, 23″) from cast-on edge, ending with a WS row. Bind off all stitches loosely.

YARN: Berroco, Denim Silk (105 yards / 50g ball)
FIBER CONTENT: 20% Silk / 80% Rayon
COLORS: A: 1429; B: 1427
AMOUNT: A: 5 (7, 8) balls; B: 1 ball
TOTAL YARDAGE: A: 525 (735, 840) yards; B: 105 yards
GAUGE: 5 stitches = 1 inch; 20 stitches = 4 inches
NEEDLE SIZE: US 7 (4.5mm) or size needed to obtain gauge; G crochet hook
SIZES: S (M, L)
KNITTED MEASUREMENTS: Width = 16″ (18″, 20″); Length = 19″ (21″, 23″)

FINISHING:

Sew shoulder seams together. Sew side seams down, reversing the side you sew on approximately 1 inch before the bottom for the rolled edge. (For more detailed instructions, see Finishing Techniques, page 29.) With color B and a G crochet hook, work 1 row of single crochet around armholes and neck.

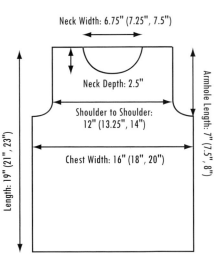

Neck Width: 6.75″ (7.25″, 7.5″)

Neck Depth: 2.5″

Shoulder to Shoulder: 12″ (13.25″, 14″)

Armhole Length: 7″ (7.5″, 8″)

Length: 19″ (21″, 23″)

Chest Width: 16″ (18″, 20″)

the same...
but
different

Do you find yourself going back to the same pattern to make the same gifts for different people? Well, Julie loved this pattern because the tanks fit her perfectly, she loved the shape and the neckline, but this time she wanted something a little different. After many discussions, Julie decided to add a lace stitch to the bottom and across the center. The lace detail added the finesse she was looking for and, in keeping with the great pattern shape, fit her perfectly. It was a little bit different from her usual—but still the same.

PATTERN STITCH:

Row 1: (WS) Knit.

Row 2: (RS) K1 *(YO, P2tog)*, end K1.

Rows 3, 4 & 5: Purl.

Row 6: As row 2.

Rows 7, 8 & 9: Purl.

BACK:

Note: The pattern stitch in the center should fall below your bust. You can change its placement to fit your body shape by placing it a few inches higher or lower than we suggest.

With #5 needle, cast on 78 (88, 98) stitches. Work in pattern stitch for 9 rows. Change to #6 needle and on row 10 begin working in St st with a knit row. Continue working in St st until piece measures 8″ (9″, 10″) from the cast-on edge, ending with a RS row. Change to #5 needle and work rows 1 through 5 in the pattern stitch. Change to #6 needle and continue to work in St st, beginning with a knit row, until piece measures 13.5″ (15″, 16″) from cast-on edge, ending with a WS row. SHAPE ARMHOLES: Bind off 4 stitches at the beginning of the next 2 rows 0 (0, 1) times. Bind off 3 stitches at the beginning of the following 2 rows. Bind off 2 stitches at the beginning of the following 2 rows. Then decrease 1 stitch at each edge every other row 4 (6, 5) times until 60 (66, 70) stitches remain. *(See step-by-step instructions on page 156.)* Continue working in St st until piece measures 20″ (22″, 24″) from cast-on edge, ending with a WS row. Bind off all stitches loosely.

FRONT:

Work as for back until piece measures 13.5″ (15″, 16″) from cast-on edge, ending with a WS row. SHAPE ARMHOLES: Bind off 4 stitches at the beginning of the next 2 rows 0 (0, 1) times. Bind off 3 stitches at the beginning of the following 2 rows. Bind off 2 stitches at the beginning of the following 2 rows. Then

decrease 1 stitch at each edge every other row 4 (6, 5) times until 60 (66, 70) stitches remain. *(See step-by-step instructions on page 156.)* Continue working in St st until piece measures 17.5″ (19.5″, 21.5″) from cast-on edge, ending with a WS row. SHAPE CREW NECK: Bind off center 18 (20, 22) stitches and then begin working each side of the neck separately. At the beginning of each neck edge, every other row, bind off 3 stitches 1 time, 2 stitches 1 time, 1 stitch 3 times. *(See step-by-step instructions on page 156.)* Continue to work on remaining 13 (15, 16) stitches with no further decreasing until piece measures 20″ (22″, 24″) from cast-on edge, ending with a WS row. Bind off all stitches loosely.

FINISHING:

Sew shoulder seams together. Sew side seams down. (For more detailed instructions, see Finishing Techniques, page 29.) ARMHOLE BANDS: With circular 16″ #5 needle, pick up 74 (78, 82) stitches around each armhole. Work as follows:

Row 1: Purl.

Rows 2 & 3: Knit.

Bind off all stitches loosely, purlwise. NECK BAND: With circular 16″ #5 needle, pick up 80 (82, 84) stitches around neck and work in pattern for 1 repeat as follows:

Rows 1 & 2: Purl.

Row 3: K1 *(YO, P2tog)*, end K1.

Row 4: Knit.

Row 5: Purl. Bind off all stitches loosely, purlwise.

YARN: Berroco, Cotton Twist (85 yards / 50g ball)
FIBER CONTENT: 70% Mercerized Cotton / 30% Rayon
COLOR: 8464
AMOUNT: 6 (8, 9) balls
TOTAL YARDAGE: 510 (680, 765) yards
GAUGE: 5 stitches = 1 inch; 20 stitches = 4 inches
NEEDLE SIZE: US 6 (4mm) for body or size needed to obtain gauge; US 5 (3.75mm) for pattern stitch; circular 16″ US 5 (3.75mm)
SIZES: S (M, L)
KNITTED MEASUREMENTS: Width = 15.5″ (17.5″, 19.5″); Length = 20″ (22″, 24″)

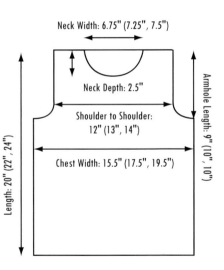

Neck Width: 6.75″ (7.25″, 7.5″)

Neck Depth: 2.5″

Armhole Length: 9″ (10″, 10″)

Shoulder to Shoulder: 12″ (13″, 14″)

Chest Width: 15.5″ (17.5″, 19.5″)

Length: 20″ (22″, 24″)

tara's tank

After her first year of knitting hats, scarves, blankets, sweaters, and tank tops in either stockinette or garter stitch, Tara was starting to get a little bored and wanted to learn something new. We designed this tank just for her. The cable down the front provided just the challenge she was looking for. And the stockinette stitch border that is knit into the V-neck was a little something extra we threw in just to keep her on her toes.

PATTERN STITCHES:

C6B = Slip 3 stitches onto a cable needle, hold at back of work, knit 3 stitches from left needle, knit 3 from cable needle.

FC = Slip 3 stitches onto a cable needle, hold at front, purl 1 stitch from left needle, knit 3 from cable needle.

BC = Slip 1 stitch onto a cable needle, hold at back, knit 3 stitches from left needle, purl 1 stitch from cable needle.

BACK:

With #10.5 needle, cast on 52 (58, 64) stitches. Work in K2, P2 ribbing for 6 rows as follows:

For Small & Large: K2, P2 every row.

For Medium:

Row 1: K2 *P2, K2* to end.

Row 2: P2 *K2, P2* to end.

For all sizes: Change to #11 needle and work in St st until piece measures 13.5″ (14.5″, 15.5″) from cast-on edge, ending with a WS row. SHAPE ARMHOLES: Bind off 3 stitches at the beginning of the next 2 rows. Bind off 2 stitches at the beginning of the following 2 rows. Then decrease 1 stitch at each edge every other row 1 (2, 2) time until 40 (44, 50) stitches remain. *(See step-by-step instructions on page 157.)* Continue working in St st until piece measures 20″ (21.5″, 23.5″) from cast-on edge, ending with a WS row. Bind off all stitches loosely.

FRONT:

Work as for back until you have completed 6 rows of ribbing. Change to #11 needle and work pattern as follows:

Row 1: K19 (22, 25), P1, K3, P6, K3, P1, K19 (22, 25).

Row 2: P19 (22, 25), K1, P3, K6, P3, K1, P19 (22, 25).

Row 3: K19 (22, 25), P1, FC, P4, BC, P1, K19 (22, 25).

Row 4: P19 (22, 25), K2, P3, K4, P3, K2, P19 (22, 25).

Row 5: K19 (22, 25), P2, FC, P2, BC, P2, K19 (22, 25).

Row 6: P19 (22, 25), K3, P3, K2, P3, K3, P19 (22, 25).

Row 7: K19 (22, 25), P3, FC, BC, P3, K19 (22, 25).

Row 8: P19 (22, 25), K4, P6, K4, P19 (22, 25).

Row 9: K19 (22, 25), P4, C6B, P4, K19 (22, 25).

Row 10: P19 (22, 25), K4, P6, K4, P19 (22, 25).

Row 11: K19 (22, 25), P3, BC, FC, P3, K19 (22, 25).

Row 12: P19 (22, 25), K3, P3, K2, P3, K3, P19 (22, 25).

Row 13: K19 (22, 25), P2, BC, P2, FC, P2, K19 (22, 25).

Row 14: P19 (22, 25), K2, P3, K4, P3, K2, P19 (22, 25).

Row 15: K19 (22, 25), P1, BC, P4, FC, P1, K19 (22, 25).

Row 16: P19 (22, 25), K1, P3, K6, P3, K1, P19 (22, 25).

Repeat this 16-row pattern until piece measures 13.5″ (14.5″, 15.5″) from cast-on edge, ending with a WS row. SHAPE ARMHOLES: Bind off 3 stitches at the beginning of the next 2 rows. Bind off 2 stitches at the beginning of the following 2 rows. Then decrease 1 stitch at each edge every other row 1 (2, 2) times until 40 (44, 50) stitches remain. *(See step-by-step instructions on page 157.)* Continue working in pattern until piece measures approximately 15″ from cast-on edge. You must begin the V-neck shaping after row 10 has been worked. SHAPE V-NECK: Place a marker at the center.

Row 1: Knit until 9 stitches before the marker, K2tog, P4, K3. Turn work around as though you were at the end of the row. You are going to ignore the rest of the stitches.

Row 2: P3, K4, purl to end of the row.

Repeat rows 1 & 2 9 (10, 11) more times until 10 (11, 13) stitches remain. *(See step-by-step instructions on page 157.)* Continue to work on these stitches until piece measures 20″ (21.5″, 23.5″) from cast-on edge, ending with a WS row. Bind off all stitches loosely.

Attach yarn to other side. You should be on a RS row.

Row 1: K3, P4, SSK, knit until end.

Row 2: Purl until 7 stitches remain, K4, P3.

Repeat rows 1 & 2 9 (10, 11) more times until 10 (11, 13) stitches remain. *(See step-by-step instructions on page 157.)* Continue to work on these stitches until piece measures 20″ (21.5″, 23.5″) from cast-on edge, ending with a WS row. Bind off all stitches loosely.

FINISHING:

Sew shoulder seams together. Sew up side seams. (See Finishing Techniques, page 29.) With a J crochet hook work 1 row of single crochet around armhole edges. (See Finishing Touches, page 36.)

YARN: Prism, Diana (60 yards / 50g ball)
FIBER CONTENT: 100% Rayon
COLOR: Denim
AMOUNT: 7 (8, 9) balls
TOTAL YARDAGE: 420 (480, 540) yards
GAUGE: 3.5 stitches = 1 inch; 14 stitches = 4 inches
NEEDLE SIZE: US 11 (8mm) or size needed to obtain gauge; US 10.5 (7mm) for ribbing; J crochet hook
SIZES: S (M, L)
KNITTED MEASUREMENTS: Width = 15″ (16.5″, 18″); Length = 20″ (21.5″, 23.5″)
Note: This yarn has a lot of give. These measurements may seem small, but the yarn stretches.

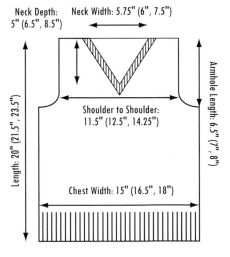

Neck Depth: 5″ (6.5″, 8.5″) Neck Width: 5.75″ (6″, 7.5″)

Length: 20″ (21.5″, 23.5″)

Armhole Length: 6.5″ (7″, 8″)

Shoulder to Shoulder: 11.5″ (12.5″, 14.25″)

Chest Width: 15″ (16.5″, 18″)

ponchos

Ponchos are hippy throwbacks that came back in vogue with a vengeance. Their recent spike in popularity aside, ponchos have long been fun projects to make because they allow knitters to show off their skills and personality. Color, texture, length, and neckline change the look of a poncho dramatically. This chapter offers four poncho patterns in timeless styles that are totally easy to customize. Plus, they're so comfortable to wear, you'll want to experiment with different yarn fibers in a variety of weights so you can wear them year-round! The pattern for the ultra-chic Hip and Hooded calls for stockinette stitch and some simple decreasing. The two easy-to-knit front and back pieces plus a hood come together for an updated and slightly fitted look. Anatomy of a Poncho is essentially one jumbo-size scarf with one edge sewn together. It hangs with one point in front while the back edge goes straight across the back. Suzanne the Visionary is knit in a star-stitch pattern (P3tog and yarn over) to give it a slightly open look. You can stripe it like we did or knit it in a solid color—either way the cool stitch will make you the envy of every girl. So Many Ponchos, So Little Time has a very classic look with a cable running up the center leading to a high turtleneck. Very soft and luxurious, it will keep you cozy on those chilly fall days. Have fun and experiment!

Looking for a hooded poncho that is supersoft and easy to make? So was Sarabeth. She found her perfect poncho at one of her favorite boutiques. She looked at the price tag, gasped, and said, "Oh, what the heck, I can return it." Moments later, Sarabeth was at our store. "Here it is," she said excitedly. "Make me a pattern." So we chose a soft alpaca yarn and wrote this pattern. The next week she came in wearing it and said, "Ladies, I love it, love it, love it! It's hip, it's hooded, and I'm happy!" It's always nice to have a satisfied customer.

BACK:

With #10 needle and 2 strands of yarn, cast on 120 (126, 134) stitches. Work in K2, P2 ribbing for 2". Change to #10.5 needle and begin to work in St st, decreasing 28 stitches evenly across the 1st row of St st. You will have 92 (98, 106) stitches. Work in St st and **at the same time** double decrease at each end of every 8th row 9 (10, 11) times. You will have 56 (58, 62) stitches, and your piece should measure approximately 20" (22", 24"). Then continue to work in St st and **at the same time** double decrease at each end every other row 8 (8, 9) times. You will have 24 (26, 26) stitches remaining. Bind off all stitches loosely.

FRONT:

Work as for back until piece measures 15" (16.5", 18") from cast-on edge, ending with a WS row. Bind off the center 6 stitches. *(See step-by-step instructions on page 157.)* Then, working each side separately, continue working in St st with the decreases on the outside edge as for the back. When piece measures 21.5" (23.5", 25.5"), S H A P E N E C K: Bind off 3 stitches twice, 2 stitches once, 1 stitch 1 (2, 2) times. *(See step-by-step instructions on page 157.)* Don't forget that you will still be working the outside edge decreases as for the back.

Note: No stitches should remain when you are done with all the decreases and the neck shaping. Repeat the neck shaping on the other side.

HOOD:

With #10.5 needle and 2 strands of yarn, cast on 24 (26, 28) stitches. Work in St st until piece measures 22" (23.5", 25") from the cast-on edge. Bind off all stitches loosely.

YARN: Blue Sky Alpaca, Alpaca (110 yards / 50g ball)
FIBER CONTENT: 100% Alpaca
COLOR: 10
AMOUNT: 10 (12, 14) balls
TOTAL YARDAGE: 1100 (1320, 1540) yards
GAUGE: **Stitch Gauge:** 3.5 stitches = 1 inch; 14 stitches = 4 inches
   Row Gauge: 4 rows = 1 inch; 16 rows = 4 inches
NEEDLE SIZE: US 10.5 (7mm) for body or size needed to obtain gauge; US 10 (6mm) for ribbing
SIZES: S (M, L)
KNITTED MEASUREMENTS: Width = 26" (28", 30"); Length = 23.5" (25.5", 27")
Yarn is worked double throughout—this means you should hold 2 strands of yarn together as though they are 1.

FINISHING:

Sew both sides of the poncho together. Fold hood in half and sew down the back side. Sew hood into neck of poncho. (For more detailed instructions, see Finishing Techniques, page 29.) With #10 needle, 2 strands of yarn, and RS facing you, pick up 112 (116, 116) stitches up neck and hood edges. Work in K2, P2 ribbing for 2". Fold ribbing in half and tack down on the inside. M A K E 2 B R A I D S A S F O L L O W S: Cut 6 20" strands of yarn. Braid them together, using 2 strands for each part of the braid. When braid measures 12" long, make a knot, leaving about 1.5" of yarn hanging for the tassel. Attach each braid at the neck seam before the ribbing.

anatomy of a poncho

With eight million people living in New York City, the odds of encountering a stranger on the train more than once is rare. One day, Julie was on the subway, sitting across from a woman wearing a terrific poncho. The simple poncho was knit in a pretty straightforward stitch, but it was unique because it was constructed in just one piece, like a large scarf, and sewn in a fashion that resulted in a poncho. Julie stared at the woman for what seemed like an eternity, trying to figure out the intricacies of the poncho. As the woman got off the train at her stop, Julie yelled, "Great poncho," and then the woman was gone. Her poncho, however, was re-created by Julie days later, and here it is for your knitting pleasure.

YARN: Filatura Di Crosa, Zara
(136 yards / 50g ball)
FIBER CONTENT: 100% Merino Wool
COLOR: 1732
AMOUNT: 10 (12, 14) balls
TOTAL YARDAGE: 1360 (1632, 1904)
yards
GAUGE: 4 stitches = 1 inch;
16 stitches = 4 inches
NEEDLE SIZE: US 10.5 (7mm) or size
needed to obtain gauge
SIZES: S (M, L)
KNITTED MEASUREMENTS: Width = 18″
(20″, 22″); Length = 42″ (46″, 52″)
Yarn is worked double throughout the
poncho—this means you should
hold 2 strands of yarn together as
though they are 1.

PATTERN STITCH:

Row 1: K1, P1 to end.

Row 2: Purl.

Repeat rows 1 & 2 to form pattern stitch.

PONCHO:

With #10.5 needle and 2 strands of yarn, cast on 72 (80, 88) stitches and work in pattern stitch until the piece measures 42″ (46″, 52″). Bind off all stitches loosely.

FINISHING:

Sew seam together as shown in diagram below, sewing AB side to DE. (For more detailed instructions, see Finishing Techniques, page 29.)

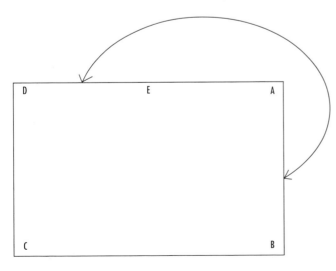

suzanne the visionary

After knitting several simple ponchos, Suzanne, the Yarn Company's manager, wanted to make something out of the ordinary. She combed through several stitch books and finally came upon this funky stitch, which looks much more difficult than it is. Later that night, as she tested out the stitch with various scrap yarn, she realized that not only was this a cool stitch in one color, but that it looked awesome in three colors. She came back to work the next day and began playing with colors. Ultimately she chose this terrific combination and said we could use the pattern for our book as long as we gave her credit—so, thanks, Suzanne!

PATTERN STITCH:

Row 1: Using color A, knit.

Row 2: Using color A, K1 *P3 together leaving stitches on left needle, YO, purl same 3 stitches together again and slip off the left needle, K1* repeat from * to * across row.

Row 3: Using color B, knit.

Row 4: Using color B, K1, P1, K1 *P3 together leaving stitches on left needle, YO, purl same 3 stitches together again and slip off the left needle, K1* repeat from * to * across row to last 2 stitches, end P1, K1.

Rows 5 & 6: Using color C, repeat rows 1 & 2.

Rows 7 & 8: Using color A, repeat rows 3 & 4.

Rows 9 & 10: Using color B, repeat rows 1 & 2.

Rows 11 & 12: Using color C, repeat rows 3 & 4.

Repeat rows 1 through 12.

FRONT AND BACK:
(make 2 pieces)

With #17 needle and color A, cast on 41 (45, 49) stitches. Work in pattern stitch until piece measures 27" (30", 34"). End with color B or C. Bind off all stitches loosely.

FINISHING:

Sew together as shown in the diagram below, making sure that the cast-on edge is the short end that is sewn to the other piece. With N crochet hook and color A, work 1 row single and then 1 row shrimp stitch around all edges. (For more detailed instructions, see Finishing Techniques, page 29.)

YARN: Tahki, Baby
(60 yards / 100g ball)
FIBER CONTENT: 100% Merino Wool
COLORS: A: 17; B: 18; C: 1
AMOUNT: A: 3 (4, 5) balls; B: 3 (4, 5) balls; C: 3 (4, 5) balls
TOTAL YARDAGE: 540 (720, 900) yards
GAUGE: 2.5 stitches = 1 inch; 10 stitches = 4 inches
NEEDLE SIZE: US 17 (12mm) or size needed to obtain gauge; N crochet hook
SIZES: S (M, L)
KNITTED MEASUREMENTS: Width = 16" (18", 20"); Length = 27" (30", 34")

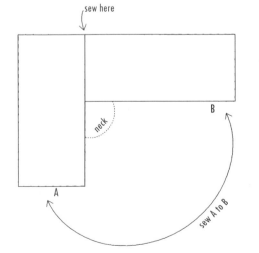

sew here

neck

A

B

sew A to B

so many ponchos, so little time

Lauren took our beginner class last year, and for her first project, she made a garter-stitch poncho. Since then, she has made numerous ponchos in garter stitch for herself, friends, and family. Eventually though, she got bored doing the same thing. We were happy to teach her something new, but there was a hitch—she only wanted to make ponchos. So we taught her how to cable. We figured it was a new technique that would look great incorporated into her ponchos. Lauren picked up the cabling technique in no time and has since made this poncho several times for herself and a few friends. She is now thinking about making a sweater . . . one of these days.

YARN: Karabella, Brushed Alpaca (35 yards / 50g ball)
FIBER CONTENT: 100% Alpaca
COLOR: 77
AMOUNT: 11 (12, 13) balls
TOTAL YARDAGE: 385 (420, 455) yards
GAUGE: 2 stitches = 1 inch;
8 stitches = 4 inches
NEEDLE SIZE: US 15 (10mm) or size needed to obtain gauge; circular 16″
SIZES: S (M, L)
KNITTED MEASUREMENTS: Width = 30″ (31.5″, 33″); Length = 29″ (31″, 33″)

PATTERN STITCH:

C10B: Place 5 stitches on a cable needle, hold at back of work, K5 from left needle, K5 from cable needle.

FRONT AND BACK:

(make 2 pieces)

Note: To Increase, knit into the front and back of the stitch. To Decrease, K1, K2tog, knit until 3 stitches remain, K2tog, K1.

With #15 needle, cast on 2 stitches. Work as follows:

Row 1: Inc, inc
you will now have 4 stitches

Row 2: Inc, P2, inc
you will now have 6 stitches

Row 3: Inc, K4, inc
you will now have 8 stitches

Row 4: Inc, P6, inc
you will now have 10 stitches

Row 5: Inc, K8, inc
you will now have 12 stitches

Row 6: Inc, P10, inc
you will now have 14 stitches

Row 7: Inc, P1, K10, P1, inc
you will now have 16 stitches

Row 8: Inc, K2, P10, K2, inc
you will now have 18 stitches

Place markers at either side of the center 14 stitches.

Row 9: Inc, K1, P2, C10B, P2, K1, inc
you will now have 20 stitches

Row 10: Inc, P2, K2, P10, K2, P2, inc
you will now have 22 stitches

Row 11: Inc, K3, P2, K10, P2, K3, inc
you will now have 24 stitches

Continue in this way, increasing 1 stitch at each edge of every row until you have 74 (78, 82) stitches. You will be knitting before and after the P2s on the RS rows and purling before and after the K2s on the WS rows. **At the same time,** cable every 14 rows for the entire pattern (you will cable next on row 23 and then 37, etc.).

Once you have 74 (78, 82) stitches, begin to decrease 1 stitch at each edge on every RS row until 20 stitches remain. Place these stitches on a holder. *Note: For small size, work 4 more rows on these 20 stitches and then place the stitches on a holder.*

FINISHING:

Sew front and back of poncho together from the neck down the entire decreased edge. (For more detailed instructions, see Finishing Techniques, page 29.) Slip stitches from holders onto 16″ circular #15 needle. Work in the round, in a K2, P2 ribbing for 4″. Bind off all stitches loosely.

hats

Unless you live in a place where it is warm and sunny all year or you have a lot of thick, wool-like hair that keeps your noggin warm, hats are a necessity during the winter. So, why not make a couple of fun, eye-catching ones—wearing an awesome hat is a nice consolation when you have to face the cold weather. They are also the perfect project if you haven't knit in a while, and they make great gifts because you can complete a project in only a few hours. The Gilbert Family Hat is your basic, standard-issue hat. It is knit in stockinette stitch without any edgy frills or ribbing so the edges roll up to create the brim. It is simple and fashionable—every person needs one. Toasty Ears is the perfect hat not only for keeping your head warm, but also for providing cover for your ears. To make this smart hat, you will need to know how to cast on stitches at the end of a row, but other than that, it is easy as can be. Make this hat in one color, add stripes, or use a second color to trim the hat. You don't need to follow our cue—make it your own. Dude, Where's My Hat? has a playful look due to its unique brim, which is extra thick because it is folded in half and sewn down. All you need are some increasing and decreasing skills to make this universally appealing topper. The Wedding Hat is one you'll need for the coldest of days. This super-warm cap has a cable and rib pattern, which is knit in the round, a great technique for seamless hats.

the gilbert family hat

We basically owe our career to Lisa, our friend who taught us to knit while we were in college. Last winter, Lisa, her husband Stu, and stepson Dillon wanted to avoid the frigid temperatures, stay inside, and rent movies. Lisa suggested that if they were going to be couch potatoes all weekend, they should "learn to knit and make basic hats for our upcoming ski trip." Lisa's mission was a success; she called the next day to say they had all made their hats and were ready to hit the slopes.

YARN: Colinette, Point 5 (55 yards / 100g ball)
FIBER CONTENT: 100% Pure Wool
COLOR: 104
AMOUNT: 1 (2, 2) balls
TOTAL YARDAGE: 55 (110, 110) yards
GAUGE: 2 stitches = 1 inch; 8 stitches = 4 inches
NEEDLE SIZE: US 17 (12mm) or size needed to obtain gauge
SIZES: S (M, L)
KNITTED MEASUREMENTS: Circumference: 19" (20", 21")

HAT:

With #17 needle, cast on 38 (40, 42) stitches. Work in St st until piece measures 6.5" (7", 7.5") from cast-on edge. Begin decreases as follows:

Row 1: *(K3, K2tog)* across row.

Rows 2, 4 & 6: Purl.

Row 3: *(K2, K2tog)* across row.

Row 5: *(K1, K2tog)* across row.

Cut yarn, leaving 15".

FINISHING:

With a yarn needle, thread yarn through remaining loops on the needle and sew down seam. (For more detailed instructions, see Finishing Techniques, page 29.)

toasty ears

Roz knits constantly for her two grandchildren, Julia and Marcus. She also is an avid skier and had plans to bring her grandchildren on their first skiing trip. She thought of every last detail, including a warm and toasty hat with earflaps. When she showed them to Julia and Marcus, they loved them and decided Grandma should have one, too. So we adjusted the pattern for an adult size, and before too long, they all had matching hats on the mountain.

YARN: Blue Sky Alpaca
(120 yards / 50g ball)
FIBER CONTENT: 100% Alpaca
COLORS: A: 10; B: 000; C: 100; D: 9
AMOUNT: 1 ball of each color
TOTAL YARDAGE: 480 yards
GAUGE: 4 stitches = 1 inch;
16 stitches = 4 inches
NEEDLE SIZE: US 9 (5.5mm) or size needed to obtain gauge; J crochet hook
SIZES: S (M, L)
KNITTED MEASUREMENTS:
Circumference: 19.5" (20", 21")
Yarn is worked double throughout the hat—this means you should hold 2 strands of each color together as though they are 1.

STRIPE PATTERN:

2 rows St st in color A
4 rows St st in color B
2 rows St st in color A
4 rows St st in color C
2 rows St st in color A
4 rows St st in color D
2 rows St st in color A
4 rows St st in color C
2 rows St st in color A
4 rows St st in color B

Continue in color A for the remainder of the hat.

Note: See page 28 to learn to cast on at the end of a row.

EARFLAPS (make 2):

With #9 needle and 2 strands of color A, cast on 6 (6, 8) stitches. Work in St st while increasing 1 stitch at each edge every other row 5 times until you have 16 (16, 18) stitches. Work in St st in color A until flap measures 3" (3", 3.25") from cast-on edge, ending with a WS row. Place these 16 (16, 18) stitches on a holder.

HAT:

With #9 needle and 2 strands of color A, cast on 10 (10, 11) stitches. Knit across the 16 (16, 18) stitches on the 1st holder, cast on 26 (28, 28) stitches, knit across the 16 (16, 18) stitches from the 2nd holder, cast on 10 (10, 11) more stitches. You will have a total of 78 (80, 86) stitches on the needle. Work in St st in the stripe pattern until piece measures 6" (6.5", 7") from

cast-on edge, ending with a WS row. Begin decreases as follows:

Row 1: *(K5, K2tog)* across row.

Rows 2, 4, 6 & 8: Purl.

Row 3: *(K4, K2tog)* across row.

Row 5: *(K3, K2tog)* across row.

Row 7: *(K2, K2tog)* across row.

Row 9: *(K1, K2tog)* across row.

Row 11: *(K2tog)* across row.

Cut yarn, leaving 20".

FINISHING:

Thread yarn through remaining loops and sew down seam. Weave in ends. With a J crochet hook and 2 strands of color A, work 1 row of single crochet all around edge of hat, including the earflaps. (For more detailed instructions, see Finishing Techniques, page 29.)

dude, where's my hat?

Jessica makes hats like they are going out of style. She saw this hat in our store and fell in love with its hip brim. She made her first hat just like ours, using five different color stripes. Then she made several others in various color combinations. They all looked awesome. She gave a few hats to friends, one to her sister, and kept one for herself. When her college-age brother came to visit and saw every-one in their hats, he said to her, the way only a younger brother can, "Dude, where's my hat?"

HAT:

With #7 needle and color A, cast on 90 (100) stitches. Work 4 rows in St st.

Row 5: Knit, increasing 1 stitch every 9th (10th) stitch.

Row 6 & all EVEN ROWS: Purl.

Row 7: Knit.

Row 9: Knit, increasing 1 stitch every 10th (11th) stitch.

Row 11: Knit.

Row 13: Knit, increasing 1 stitch every 11th (12th) stitch.

Row 15: Purl. **This row makes the turning ridge.**

Row 17: Knit, decreasing 1 stitch every 11th (12th) stitch.

Row 19: Knit.

Row 21: Knit, decreasing 1 stitch every 10th (11th) stitch.

Row 23: Knit.

Row 25: Knit, decreasing 1 stitch every 9th (10th) stitch.

Note: All increases should use the M1 method. All decreases should use the K2tog method.

Change to #8 needle and begin working in St st with color B. Work 10 (12) rows. Change to color C and work 10 (12) rows in St st. Change to color D and work 10 (12) rows in St st. Change to color E and begin decreases as follows:

Row 1: *(K7, K2tog)* across row.

Row 2 & all EVEN ROWS: Purl.

Row 3: *(K6, K2tog)* across row.

Row 5: *(K5, K2tog)* across row.

Row 7: *(K4, K2tog)* across row.

Row 9: *(K3, K2tog)* across row.

Change to color A on row 11 (13) and finish the hat in this color.

Row 11: *(K2, K2tog)* across row.

Row 13: *(K1, K2tog)* across row.

Row 15: *(K2tog)* across row.

Cut yarn, leaving 20".

YARN: Tahki, Donegal Tweed (176 yards / 100g ball)
FIBER CONTENT: 100% Wool
COLORS: A: 869; B: 838; C: 892; D: 894; E: 848
AMOUNT: 1 ball of each color
TOTAL YARDAGE: You can complete this hat with 350 yards
GAUGE: 4.5 stitches = 1 inch; 18 stitches = 4 inches
NEEDLE SIZE: US 8 (5mm) or size needed to obtain gauge; US 7 (4.5mm)
SIZES: S (L)
KNITTED MEASUREMENTS: Circumference: 20" (22")

FINISHING:

Thread yarn through remaining loops and sew down seam. Fold the brim at the turning ridge and tack it down on the inside edge with a separate piece of color A. (For more detailed instructions, see Finishing Techniques, page 29.)

wedding hat

Jordana and Jeff got married on a mountaintop in the middle of winter. Jeff needed to cover his head during the ceremony, but the traditional yarmulke just wasn't going to cut it in the zero-degree weather. Jordana made him this cabled hat to wear instead. Jeff received almost as many compliments on his wedding garb as Jordana! The hat was so popular, Jordana sized down the pattern for women to include it in this book.

YARN: Filatura Di Crosa, Zara (136 yards / 50g ball)
FIBER CONTENT: 100% Merino Wool
COLOR: 1719
AMOUNT: 3 balls
TOTAL YARDAGE: 408 yards
GAUGE: 3 stitches = 1 inch; 12 stitches = 4 inches
NEEDLE SIZE: Circular 16" US 10.5 (7mm) or size needed to obtain gauge; circular 16" US 9 (5mm) for ribbing
SIZES: S (L)
KNITTED MEASUREMENTS: Circumference: 19.5" (21")
Yarn is worked double throughout the hat—this means you should hold 2 strands of yarn together as though they are 1.

PATTERN STITCH:

C4B = Place 2 stitches on a cable needle. Hold them at the back of the work. Knit 2 stitches from the left needle. Knit 2 stitches from the cable needle.

Rounds 1, 2, 4, 5 & 6: *(K2, P2, K4, P2)* across row.

Round 3: *(K2, P2, C4B, P2)* across row.

HAT:

With #9 needle and 2 strands of yarn, cast on 68 (78) stitches. Place a marker at the beginning of the round and join the stitches in a circle. Make sure all stitches are facing the same way and that they are not twisted on the needle. Work in K2, P2 ribbing for 3". Increase 12 stitches evenly across last round of ribbing until you have 80 (90) stitches. Change to #10.5 needle and begin working in cable pattern until piece measures 8" (9") from cast-on edge. Begin decreases as follows:

Round 1: *(K2tog at each K2)*

Round 2: *(P2tog at each P2)*

Round 3: *(K2tog in middle of each K4)*

Cut yarn, leaving 10".

NOTE:
This pattern is worked in the round.

FINISHING:

With a darning needle, thread yarn through remaining loops on the needle and pull until the top of the hat is closed. Pull the remaining yarn through to the WS of the work and secure it.

scarves

Scarves provide knitters with the perfect opportunity to experiment. They are relatively small projects that don't require a great time commitment. Learning a new stitch or playing with different fibers is less intimidating with a scarf project than when knitting a whole sweater. With a scarf, there are no increases or decreases to contend with—just a long rectangle. Most of all, scarves are great because you really can never have too many of them—one to go with each coat, dressy ones, casual ones, warm ones, and ones that simply accessorize an outfit. Gift of the Movies is worked on giant needles and is knit in stockinette stitch. A Little Bit of Oomph is also knit on nice, big needles but introduces the technique of wrapping the yarn around the needle twice, which creates an elongated stitch. To Knit or Not to Knit uses the simple two-by-two rib stitch that you often see on the edging of sweaters. Much of its interest comes from the fibers used—the mohair combined with the hand-dyed worsted wool creates an elegant and fun effect. The Perfect Scarf is a classic—you can't go wrong with seed stitch; it is simple, yet beautiful. Seed stitch requires a bit of concentration because you are switching back and forth from knit to purl, but you eventually get into a groove.

gift of the movies

YARN: Cascade Yarns, Magnum
(123 yards / 250g ball)
FIBER CONTENT: 100% Pure New Wool
COLORS: A: 9415; B: 9407
AMOUNT: 1 ball of each color
TOTAL YARDAGE: 246 yards
GAUGE: 1.5 stitches = 1 inch;
6 stitches = 4 inches
NEEDLE SIZE: US 19 (15mm) or size
needed to obtain gauge
KNITTED MEASUREMENTS: Width = 11″;
Length = 60″

Kendra came into the shop one Saturday afternoon and told us she wanted to knit a gift for her friend who was having a birthday brunch the next day. To complicate the situation, Kendra was going to a movie that night. Jordana, who always knits during movies, suggested that Kendra use her time wisely in the movie and knit. We wrote this pattern, which is knit on gigantic needles, and told her to estimate where she needed to change the colors. Kendra later told us that she'd finished the scarf before the movie ended, and now she can't see a movie without knitting.

SCARF:

With #19 needle and color A, cast on 18 stitches. Work in St st until piece measures 6″ from cast-on edge. Change to color B and continue in St st until piece measures 30″ from cast-on edge. Change to color A and continue in St st until piece measures 54″ from cast-on edge. Change to color B and continue in St st until piece measures 60″ from cast-on edge. Bind off all stitches loosely.

a little bit of oomph

YARN: Gedifra, Byzanz
(33 yards / 50g ball)
FIBER CONTENT: 60% Acrylic / 20%
New Wool / 15% Polyamide / 5%
Polyester
COLOR: 1621
AMOUNT: 3 balls
TOTAL YARDAGE: 99 yards
GAUGE: 2 stitches = 1 inch;
8 stitches = 4 inches
NEEDLE SIZE: US 17 (12mm) or size
needed to obtain gauge
KNITTED MEASUREMENTS: Width = 6″;
Length = 50″

On a recent trip to New York, Patricia came into our store wanting to purchase lots and lots of yarns so she could knit scarves to sell in her tea shop. Patricia wanted quick projects knit in fun yarn, but did not want to make scarves in garter stitch, because it was "too boring." She said, "I want a stitch with a little oomph!" After trying out several pattern stitches that were too complicated or just didn't show up in a fun yarn, we hit upon this stitch. Even though it is mostly done in the knit stitch, the elongated stitches that are formed simply by wrapping the yarn around the needle on one row and then dropping the wraps on the next row gave the scarf just the oomph she was looking for.

SCARF:

With #17 needle, cast on 12 stitches. Work in pattern as follows:

Row 1: Knit.

Row 2: Knit.

Row 3: *K1 wrapping yarn twice around needle*, repeat from * to * across row.

Row 4: *K1 dropping wrap stitch*, repeat from * to * across row.

Repeat rows 1 through 4 until scarf measures 50″, ending with a row 2. Bind off all stitches loosely.

to knit or not to knit

Maddie came into the store, waving around the Yarn Company gift certificate her brother had bought for her. She announced, "I used to knit, so my brother thought this would be a good Christmas present. I don't really want to start knitting again, but I need to use this. Can someone help me?" Suzanne bravely stepped forward and showed Maddie some simple scarf patterns using only the knit stitch, explaining that any of these would certainly take care of the gift certificate and end her ordeal quickly. But Maddie wasn't sold. "I can't just knit; I'll be bored to death. I need a stitch." Suzanne then suggested this pattern, using fun yarns and a simple rib stitch to keep things interesting. Maddie started and finished the scarf on a flight to Los Angeles to visit her brother, and she called us as soon as she got off the plane. "I love it!" she told us, full of enthusiasm. "I'll be in next week for my next project."

YARNS: A: Manos Del Uruguay (138 yards / 100g ball); B: Katia, Ingenua (153 yards / 50g ball)
FIBER CONTENT: A: 100% Handspun Pure Wool; B: 78% Mohair / 13% Polyamide / 9% Wool
COLORS: A: 47; B: 21
AMOUNT: 2 balls of each color
TOTAL YARDAGE: A: 276 yards; B: 306 yards
GAUGE: 3 stitches = 1 inch; 12 stitches = 4 inches
NEEDLE SIZE: US 11 (8mm) or size needed to obtain gauge
KNITTED MEASUREMENTS: Width = 8"; Length = 68" (excluding fringe)
Yarn is worked double throughout the scarf—this means you should hold 1 strand of A and 1 strand of B together as though they are 1.

SCARF:

With #11 needle and 1 strand of yarn A and 1 strand of yarn B, cast on 24 stitches. Work in K2, P2 ribbing until the scarf measures 68". Bind off all stitches loosely.

FINISHING:

Cut 20" lengths of yarn B. Using 4 strands held together, attach fringe to the top and bottom of the scarf, spacing it as desired.

the perfect scarf

We suggested a seed-stitch scarf for Mikie, who wanted to knit a reversible scarf that had some texture to it. Although Mikie is a good knitter, she doesn't feel ready to rip out her own rows. So she comes in and says, "My stitch is too loose, please pull it out for me." And even though the stitches often look just fine to us, we rip them out for her and let her reknit them. Mikie probably knit every row of this scarf twice just to get it exactly so—and she nearly drove us crazy—but we laugh about it now and her scarf is certainly perfect.

YARN: Karabella, Aurora Melange (98 yards / 50g ball)
FIBER CONTENT: 100% Merino Wool
COLOR: 11
AMOUNT: 6 balls
TOTAL YARDAGE: 588 yards
GAUGE: 3 stitches = 1 inch; 12 stitches = 4 inches
NEEDLE SIZE: US 11 (8mm) or size needed to obtain gauge
KNITTED MEASUREMENTS: Width = 8"; Length = 60"
Yarn is worked double throughout the scarf—this means you should hold 2 strands of yarn together as though they are 1.

NOTE:
For seed stitch, it's easiest if your project is worked over an odd number of stitches; this way you can always start new rows with a knit stitch and concentrate even less.

SCARF:

With #11 needle and 2 strands of yarn, cast on 25 stitches. Work in seed stitch, (K1, P1) every row, until piece measures 60". Bind off all stitches loosely.

blankets

Blankets are fantastic for sprucing up or adding a finishing touch to a room. Not to mention that they are also perfect for cuddling. Many customers make blankets as a thoughtful wedding present or special birthday gift. For those intimidated by the shaping and finishing steps required for garments, a blanket is a straight shot, and best of all, it doesn't have to fit anyone. There are four blankets in this chapter. A Scarf Grows in Manhattan uses four strands of yarn held together as though they are one and is knit in garter stitch on giant needles. Nancy's Color Block Blanket is knit in strips. It is a perfect blanket project to make when traveling because it never gets too cumbersome. We used varied but simple stitches (such as seed stitch, a cable, and garter stitch) and knit each stitch pattern in one of five complementary colors. Feel free to follow our lead or use one color to let the stitches speak for themselves. Use your imagination, be creative, and have fun picking out the colors if you want to make each block a different color. The Freshman is knit in a slip-stitch pattern, which is quite easy. All you do is slip the stitch to the other needle, which is even easier than knitting. You can make a bold and fun blanket by choosing two very contrasting colors, or you can produce a more subtle effect by choosing colors with similar tone. A Family Affair has a few large cables spaced by seed stitch. It is knit with a mohair and a merino wool held together to give it a soft, fuzzy look.

a scarf grows in manhattan

This pattern has a long history with the Yarn Company, having gone through two transformations. It all began a few years ago when Jordana had the idea to hold together four yarn strands in different colors and knit them in garter stitch to make a scarf. Our customers loved it, not only because it was quick to knit on giant needles, but because they could choose their own colors to blend together. One customer, Tara, then transformed the scarf pattern into a baby blanket and made them for all of her friends' babies. We liked it so much as a baby blanket that we included the pattern in our kids' book. We got such a great response from our clientele, we decided to morph the pattern yet again into an adult-size afghan. We think it is perfect to throw over your couch or chair, and you can choose your colors to match your room. It is also superfast, superwarm, and supersoft.

YARN: Filatura Di Crosa, Zara (136 yards / 50g ball)
FIBER CONTENT: 100% Merino Wool
COLORS: A: 1663; B: 1451; C: 1476; D: 1477
AMOUNT: A: 10 balls; B, C & D: 9 balls each
TOTAL YARDAGE: 5032 yards
GAUGE: 2 stitches = 1 inch; 8 stitches = 4 inches
NEEDLE SIZE: US 17 (12mm) or size needed to obtain gauge; N crochet hook
KNITTED MEASUREMENTS: Width = 40"; Length = 60"
Yarn is worked quadruple throughout the blanket—this means you should hold 4 strands of yarn together as though they are 1.

BLANKET:

With #17 needle and 4 strands of yarn (one of each color), cast on 80 stitches. Work in garter stitch until piece measures 60". Bind off all stitches loosely.

FINISHING:

With N crochet hook and 4 strands of color A held together, work 1 row in single crochet and then 1 row in shrimp stitch along each of the long edges. Add fringe to the top and bottom by cutting 12" lengths of all colors and holding 8 strands together (2 of each color) for each fringe. Place the fringe where desired.

nancy's
color block
blanket

This pattern was inspired by a similar blanket that Nancy, Julie's mom, saw in an expensive home-decor shop. Nancy wanted one for her beach house but didn't want to pay the big price, so she asked Julie for her opinion. Julie saw the fancy blanket and knew it would take Nancy years to finish an identical blanket because the stitches were very intricate and the yarn was very thin. So, Julie redesigned the blanket for her mom using thicker yarns and simple yet striking stitches. Nancy finished her blanket in just a few months, and Julie liked it so much she knew it would be a great pattern for this book.

YARN: Crystal Palace Yarns, Chenille (98 yards / 50g ball)
FIBER CONTENT: 100% Cotton
COLORS: A: 5800; B: 5137; C: 6130; D: 8133; E: 3417
AMOUNT: A: 9 balls; B, C, D & E: 6 balls each
TOTAL YARDAGE: 3234 yards
GAUGE: 2.75 stitches = 1 inch; 11 stitches = 4 inches
NEEDLE SIZE: US 10.5 (7mm) or size needed to obtain gauge
KNITTED MEASUREMENTS: Width = 40"; Length = 60"
Yarn is worked double throughout the blanket—this means you should hold 2 strands of yarn together as though they are 1.

COLOR A—PATTERN STITCH #1:

(worked over 23 stitches)

Row 1: (RS) Knit.

Row 2: (WS) Purl.

Repeat rows 1 & 2 until pattern measures 4", ending with a WS.

Row 3: (RS) K7, P9, K7.

Row 4: (WS) P7, K9, P7.

Repeat rows 3 & 4 until pattern measures 8", ending with a WS row.

Then repeat rows 1 & 2 until pattern measures 12", ending with a WS row.

COLOR B—PATTERN STITCH #2:

(worked over 23 stitches)

Row 1: (RS) Knit.

Row 2: (WS) Purl.

Rows 3 through 7: Knit.

Rows 8 & 10: Purl.

Row 9: Knit.

Repeat rows 1 through 10 to form garter ridge pattern until pattern measures 12", ending with a WS row.

COLOR C—PATTERN STITCH #3:

(worked over 24 stitches)

Increase 1 stitch on the first row of this pattern so that you have 24 stitches.

Row 1: (RS) Knit.

Row 2: (WS) K4, P4.

Rows 3, 4 & 5: K4, P4.

Rows 6, 7, 8 & 9: P4, K4.

Repeat rows 2 through 9 until pattern measures 12", ending with a RS row, preferably a row 5 or 9.

COLOR D—PATTERN STITCH #4:

(worked over 26 stitches)

Row 1: (WS) Purl.

Row 2: (RS) P10, inc 1, K4, inc 1, P10. **Only do these increases the first time you work a row 2; on all other row 2's work as rows 5, 7 & 9.**

Row 3: (WS) K10, P6, K10.

Row 4: P10, C6B (place 3 stitches on a cable needle, hold at back of work, K3 stitches from left needle, K3 stitches from the cable needle), P10.

Rows 5, 7 & 9: P10, K6, P10.

Rows 6 & 8: As row 3.

Repeat rows 2 through 9 until pattern measures 12", ending with a WS row.

COLOR E—PATTERN STITCH #5:

(worked over 23 stitches)

Row 1: Knit, decreasing 3 stitches evenly across this row. **Do not do row 1 when you begin a strip with Pattern E.**

All other rows: K1, P1 every row until pattern measures 12".

strip 1	strip 2	strip 3	strip 4	strip 5
5	1	2	3	4
4	5	1	2	3
3	4	5	1	2
2	3	4	5	1
1	2	3	4	5

BLANKET:

The blanket is worked in 5 strips that each have 5 different patterns. Each strip is 8" wide by 60" long. Each pattern is always worked in the same color as noted above in the pattern-stitch notes.

STRIP #1:

With 2 strands of color A, cast on 23 stitches and work in the following sequence: Pattern stitch #1, pattern stitch #2, pattern stitch #3, pattern stitch #4, pattern stitch #5. Bind off.

STRIP #2:

With 2 strands of color B, cast on 23 stitches and work in the following sequence: Pattern stitch #2, pattern stitch #3, pattern stitch #4, pattern stitch #5, pattern stitch #1. Bind off.

STRIP #3:

With 2 strands of color C, cast on 24 stitches and work in the following sequence: Pattern stitch #3, pattern stitch #4, pattern stitch #5, pattern stitch #1, pattern stitch #2. Bind off.

STRIP #4:

With 2 strands of color D, cast on 26 stitches and work in the following sequence: Pattern stitch #4, pattern stitch #5, pattern stitch #1, pattern stitch #2, pattern stitch #3. Bind off.

STRIP #5:

With 2 strands of color E, cast on 23 stitches and work in the following sequence: Pattern stitch #5, pattern stitch #1, pattern stitch #2, pattern stitch #3, pattern stitch #4. Bind off.

FINISHING:

Sew strips together. With #10.5 needle, 2 strands of color A, and RS facing you, pick up 118 stitches across top of blanket. Work 6 rows in garter stitch and then bind off all stitches. Repeat this for the bottom of the blanket. (For more detailed instructions, see Finishing Techniques, page 29.)

With #10.5 needle, 2 strands of color A, and RS facing you, pick up 225 stitches up side edge. Work 6 rows in garter stitch and then bind off all stitches loosely. Repeat this for the other side.

the freshman

Janet wanted to make a blanket that her daughter, Charlotte, could take to college her freshman year. Charlotte was very picky about her dorm room decorations, and she wanted this blanket to be just so. Janet was a little nervous about taking on a big blanket, so she wanted to make sure that it wasn't too difficult, but she also didn't want to get bored. We found this stitch that met both mother's and daughter's approval. It is an easy slip-stitch pattern that looks like it requires a lot of work when actually it doesn't. Charlotte's blanket turned out fantastically. It goes perfectly in her room and, best of all, she uses it all the time. None of her girlfriends can believe that her mother knit it.

YARN: Manos del Uruguay (138 yards / 100g ball)
FIBER CONTENT: 100% Handspun Pure Wool
COLORS: A: M; B: 24
AMOUNT: A: 8 balls; B: 9 balls
TOTAL YARDAGE: 2346 yards
GAUGE: 4.5 stitches = 1 inch; 18 stitches = 4 inches
NEEDLE SIZE: US 10.5 (7mm) and US 11 (8mm) or size needed to obtain gauge
KNITTED MEASUREMENTS: Width = 36″; Length = 60″

PATTERN STITCH:

Note: Slip all stitches purlwise. Yarn is stranded on the RS.

Row 1: With color B: K2, *with yarn in front (wyif), slip 2 stitches, K2; repeat from * to last 2 stitches, K2.

Row 2: K2, *P2, with yarn in back (wyib), slip 2 stitches; repeat from * to last 2 stitches, K2.

Row 3: With color A: K2, *K2, wyif, slip 2 stitches; repeat from * to last 2 stitches, K2.

Row 4: K2, *wyib, slip 2 stitches, P2; repeat from * to last 2 stitches, K2.

BLANKET:

With #10.5 needle and color A, cast on 120 stitches. Knit 12 rows, increasing 28 stitches evenly across the last knit row, so that you have 148 stitches. Change to #11 needle and begin to work in pattern stitch until piece measures 58″ from cast-on edge, ending with a row 4 of the pattern. Change to #10.5 needle and color A and decrease 28 stitches evenly across the next row so that you have 120 stitches. Knit 11 more rows. Bind off all stitches loosely.

FINISHING:

Decide which side you like best; either one can be the RS. Then with the RS facing, a #10.5 needle, and color A, pick up 202 stitches along side edge and knit 12 rows. Bind off all stitches loosely. Repeat this step along the other side edge.

a family affair

David's mother, Barbara, offered to knit him a throw as a house-warming present. She told him to come to our store and pick out the yarn and a pattern and she would make it. David came with his whole family in tow, and everyone had an opinion as to what the blanket should look like. Betsy, his wife, is a traditionalist and wanted to keep it simple. "One color," she said adamantly. Adam, their thirteen-year-old son, put his two cents in, saying, "It has to be soft." Cleo, who is seven, said, "I like those squiggly things." And David said he wanted it to have some texture. After much contemplation we chose a beautiful color in a very soft combination of yarns. It has three cables, the squiggles Cleo wanted, and the wonderful seed-stitch texture between the cables. Barbara made it, and it looks wonderful on the couch.

YARNS: A: Unique Kolours, Mohair (185 yards / 100g ball); B: Filatura Di Crosa, Zara (136 yards / 50g ball)
FIBER CONTENT: A: 78% Mohair / 13% Wool / 9% Nylon; B: 100% Merino Wool
COLORS: A: 113; B: 1503
AMOUNT: A: 8 balls; B: 11 balls
TOTAL YARDAGE: A: 1480 yards; B: 1496 yards
GAUGE: 3 stitches = 1 inch; 12 stitches = 4 inches
NEEDLE SIZE: US 11 (8mm) or size needed to obtain gauge
KNITTED MEASUREMENTS: Width = 40"; Length = 60"
Yarn is worked double throughout the blanket—this means you should hold 1 strand of A and 1 strand of B together as though they are 1.

PATTERN STITCH:

C10B = Place 5 stitches on cable needle, hold at the back of the work, knit 5 from the left needle, knit 5 from the cable needle.

BLANKET:

With #11 needle and 1 strand of A and 1 strand of B, cast on 117 stitches. Work in seed stitch for 12 rows as follows: K1, P1 every row. Then work in pattern as follows:

Row 1: (RS) K1, (P1, K1) 5 times, *K10, P1, (K1, P1) 3 times, K10, K1, (P1, K1) 3 times* repeat from * to * 1 more time, end K10, P1, (K1, P1) 3 times, K10, (K1, P1) 5 times, K1.

Rows 2, 4, 6, 8, 10, 12, 14 & 16: (WS) K1, (P1, K1) 5 times, *P10, P1 (K1, P1) 3 times, P10, K1, (P1, K1) 3 times* repeat from * to * 1 more time, end P10, P1, (K1, P1) 3 times, P10, (K1, P1) 5 times, K1.

Rows 3, 7, 9, 11, 13 & 15: As row 1.

Row 5: K1, (P1, K1) 5 times, *C10B, P1, (K1, P1) 3 times, K10, K1, (P1, K1) 3 times * repeat from * to * 1 more time, end C10B, P1, (K1, P1) 3 times, C10B, (K1, P1) 5 times, K1.

Repeat rows 1 through 16 until piece measures 58" from cast-on edge, ending with a WS row. Work in seed stitch for 12 rows as follows: K1, P1 every row. Bind off all stitches loosely.

RESOURCES

Yarns used in this book can be ordered directly through the Yarn Company. However, yarns change seasonally and it is possible that some of the yarns may not be available when you're ready to place an order. Remember, you do not have to use the exact yarns we used in order to get great results. Just choose a yarn or a combination of yarns that gets the required gauge. You can also contact the manufacturer or search online for local retailers. The following is a list of all the distributors whose yarns were used in this book.

THE YARN COMPANY
2274 Broadway
New York, NY 10024
(212) 787-7878
(888) YARNCO1
www.theyarnco.com

ARTFUL YARNS
JCA, Inc.
35 Scales Lane
Townsend, MA 01469
(800) 225-6340

BERROCO YARNS
Berroco, Inc.
14 Elmdale Road
P.O. Box 367
Uxbridge, MA 01569
(800) 343-4948
www.berroco.com

BLUE SKY ALPACA YARNS
Blue Sky Alpaca, Inc.
P.O. Box 387
St. Francis, MN 55070
(888) 460-8862
www.blueskyalpacas.com

CASCADE YARNS
Cascade Yarns, Inc.
P.O. Box 58168
Tukwila, WA 98138
(206) 574-0440
www.cascadeyarns.com

CLASSIC ELITE YARNS
Classic Elite Yarns
300 Jackson Street
Lowell, MA 01852
(978) 453-2837
www.classiceliteyarns.com

CRYSTAL PALACE YARNS
Crystal Palace
160 23rd Street
Richmond, CA 94804
(800) 666-7455
www.straw.com

FILATURA DI CROSA & TAHKI YARNS
Tahki/Stacy Charles, Inc.
7030 80th Street, Building #36
Floor 1
Glendale, NY 11385
(800) 338-9276
www.tahkistacycharles.com

GGH YARNS
Muench Yarns, Inc.
1323 Scott Street
Petaluma, CA 94954
(800) 733-9276
www.muenchyarns.com

KARABELLA YARNS
Karabella Yarns, Inc.
1201 Broadway
New York, NY 10001
(212) 684-2665
www.karabellayarns.com

KNIT ONE, CROCHET TOO YARNS
Knit One, Crochet Too, Inc.
7 Commons Avenue, Suite 2
Windham, ME 04062
(800) 357-7646
www.knitonecrochettoo.com

MANOS DEL URUGUAY YARNS
Design Source
P.O. Box 770
Medford, MA 02155
(888) 566-9970

NORO, GEDIFRA, KATIA & ONLINE YARNS
Knitting Fever/Euro Yarns
P.O. Box 502
Roosevelt, NY 11575
(800) 645-3457
www.knittingfever.com

PRISM YARNS
Prism Yarns, Inc.
3140 39th Avenue North
Saint Petersburg, FL 33714
(727) 327-3100
www.prismyarn.com

ROWAN YARNS
Westminster Fibers, Inc.
4 Townsend W., Suite 8
Nashua, NH 03063
(800) 445-9276
www.knitrowan.com

APPENDIX
STEP-BY-STEP INSTRUCTIONS FOR ALL PROJECTS

CREWNECK AND FUNNEL-NECK PULLOVERS

Basic Instinct

SHAPING THE ARMHOLES:

Row 1: Bind off 4 stitches. Knit to end of the row.
Row 2: Bind off 4 stitches. Purl to end of the row.
Row 3: Bind off 3 stitches. Knit to end of the row.
Row 4: Bind off 3 stitches. Purl to end of the row.
Row 5: K2, SSK, knit to last 4 stitches, K2tog, K2.
Row 6: Purl.
Repeat rows 5 and 6 1 (2, 4) more time.

SHAPING THE NECK:

Remember that after binding off the center stitches, you will work 1 side at a time.
Row 1: St st for 23 (25, 26) stitches; with the 22nd (24th, 25th) stitch begin to bind off the center 18 (20, 22) stitches. For example, for the small size, this means you should pull the 22nd stitch over the 23rd stitch, and this is your first bind-off. When you are done binding off the center 18 (20, 22) stitches, check to make sure you have 21 (23, 24) stitches on each side of the hole, including the stitch on the right needle. Knit to the end of the row.
Rows 2, 4, 6, 8 & 10: Purl.
Row 3: Bind off 3 stitches. Knit to end of the row.
Row 5: Bind off 2 stitches. Knit to end of the row.

Row 7: Bind off 1 stitch. Knit to end of the row.
Row 9: Bind off 1 stitch. Knit to end of the row.
When you are done with the bind-off instructions, measure the length of the front piece, comparing it to the length of the back. If the front and back measure the same, bind off the remaining stitches. If the front is too short, continue knitting and purling until the pieces are of equal length, then bind off.

For the other side of the neck edge, attach yarn to the remaining stitches at the center of the work (not at the side edge) and begin binding off stitches immediately. You will now be binding off with a WS row facing you. Finish neck shaping as on other side, but purling to the end of the row and knitting the even-numbered rows.

Indulge Yourself

SHAPING THE A-LINE:

Row 1: K2, SSK, knit until 4 stitches remain, K2tog, K2.
Rows 2, 4 & 6: Purl.
Rows 3 & 5: Knit.
Repeat rows 1 through 6 7 (8, 9) more times.

SHAPING THE RAGLAN SLEEVES:

Row 1: Bind off 2 stitches. Knit to end of the row.
Row 2: Bind off 2 stitches. Purl to end of the row.
Row 3: K2, SSK, knit until 4 stitches remain, K2tog, K2.

Row 4: Purl.
Repeat rows 3 & 4 11 (13, 15) more times.

SHAPING THE FUNNEL NECK:

Rows 1 & 3: Purl.
Row 2: K2, increase 1, knit to last 2 stitches, increase 1, K2.
Row 4: Knit.
Repeat rows 1 through 4 7 more times. Bind off all stitches loosely.

Beware the Bunny

SHAPING THE ARMHOLES:

Row 1: Bind off 3 stitches. Knit to end of the row.
Row 2: Bind off 3 stitches. Purl to end of the row.
Row 3: Bind off 2 stitches. Knit to end of the row.
Row 4: Bind off 2 stitches. Purl to end of the row.
Row 5: K2, SSK, knit to last 4 stitches, K2tog, K2.
Row 6: Purl.
Repeat rows 5 & 6 3 (5, 5) more times.

SHAPING THE FUNNEL NECK:

Row 1: Bind off 8 (10, 12) stitches. Knit to end of the row.
Row 2: Bind off 8 (10, 12) stitches. Purl to end of the row.
Continue to work in St st on the remaining 22 (22, 24) stitches for 6 rows.
Bind off all stitches loosely.

Cables in Chamonix

SHAPING THE ARMHOLES:

Note:
Bind off in pattern.
Row 1: Bind off 3 stitches. Pattern to end of the row.
Row 2: Bind off 3 stitches. Pattern to end of the row.
Row 3: Bind off 2 stitches. Pattern to end of the row.
Row 4: Bind off 2 stitches. Pattern to end of the row.
Row 5: K2, SSK, pattern to last 4 stitches, K2tog, K2.
Row 6: Pattern.
Repeat rows 5 & 6 1 (2, 3) more time.

SHAPING THE CREW NECK:

Remember that after binding off the center stitches, you will work 1 side at a time.
Row 1: Work in pattern for 24 (27, 30) stitches; with the 23rd (26th, 29th) stitch begin to bind off the center 6 stitches. For example, for the small size, this means you should pull the 23rd stitch over the 24th stitch, and this is your first bind-off. When you are done binding off the center 6 stitches, check to make sure you have 22 (25, 28) stitches on each side of the hole, including the stitch on the right needle. Work in pattern to the end of the row.
Rows 2, 4, 6, 8 & 10: Work in pattern.
Row 3: Bind off 4 stitches. Pattern to end of the row.
Row 5: Bind off 3 stitches. Pattern to end of the row.
Row 7: Bind off 2 stitches. Pattern to end of the row.
Row 9: Bind off 1 stitch.

Pattern to end of the row. Repeat rows 9 & 10 0 (1, 2) more times.
When you are done with the bind-off instructions, measure the length of the front piece, comparing it to the length of the back. If the front and back measure the same, bind off the remaining stitches. If the front is too short, continue in pattern until the pieces are of equal length, then bind off.

For the other side of the neck edge, attach yarn to the remaining stitches at the center of the work (not at the side edge) and begin binding off stitches immediately. You will now be binding off with a WS row facing you. Finish neck shaping as on other side.

V-NECK PULLOVERS

Soccer Mom Sweater
Be aware that you might be shaping armhole and neck at the same time

SHAPING THE ARMHOLES:

Row 1: Bind off 2 stitches. Knit to end of the row.
Row 2: Bind off 2 stitches. Purl to end of the row.
Row 3: K2, SSK, knit to last 4 stitches, K2tog, K2.
Row 4: Purl.
Repeat rows 3 & 4 2 (3, 4) more times.

SHAPING THE V-NECK:

First you must place a marker on the needle to indicate the center of the work.

Row 1: Knit to 4 stitches before the marker, K2tog, K2.
Rows 2 & 4: Purl.
Row 3: Knit.
Repeat rows 1 through 4 2 more times. Then repeat rows 1 & 2 3 (4, 5) more times.
When you are done with the decrease instructions, measure the length of the front piece, comparing it to the back. If the front and back measure the same, bind off the remaining stitches. If the front is too short, continue knitting and purling until the pieces are of equal length, then bind off.
Attach yarn to the other side of the V-neck.
Row 1: K2, SSK, knit to end of the row.
Rows 2 & 4: Purl.
Row 3: Knit.
Repeat rows 1 through 4 2 more times. Then repeat rows 1 & 2 3 (4, 5) more times.
When you are done with the decrease instructions, measure the length of the front piece, comparing it to the back. If the front and back measure the same, bind off the remaining stitches. If the front is too short, continue knitting and purling until the pieces are of equal length, then bind off.

Even Daniele Did It, Yet Again
SHAPING THE RAGLAN ARMHOLES:

Row 1: Bind off 2 stitches. Knit to end of the row.
Row 2: Bind off 2 stitches. Purl to end of the row.
Row 3: K2, SSK, knit to last 4 stitches, K2tog, K2.
Row 4: Purl.
Repeat rows 3 & 4 19 (21, 24) more times. Bind off remaining stitches.

The Subway Cable
Be aware that you might be shaping armhole and neck at the same time

SHAPING THE ARMHOLES:

Row 1: Bind off 3 stitches. Pattern to end of the row.
Row 2: Bind off 3 stitches. Pattern to end of the row.
Row 3: Bind off 2 stitches. Pattern to end of the row.
Row 4: Bind off 2 stitches. Pattern to end of the row.
Row 5: K2, SSK, knit to last 4 stitches, K2tog, K2.
Row 6: Purl.
Repeat rows 5 & 6 2 (2, 4) more times.

SHAPING THE V-NECK:

Place a marker on the needle to indicate the center of the work.
Row 1: Knit until 10 stitches before the marker, K2tog, P2, K6.
Row 2: Knit the knit stitches and purl the purls.
Repeat rows 1 & 2 7 (8, 9) more times.
When you are done with the decrease instructions, measure the length of the front piece, comparing it to the back. If the front and back measure the same, bind off the remaining stitches. If the front is too short, continue working in pattern until the pieces are of equal length, then bind off.
Attach yarn to the other side of the V-neck.
Row 1: K6, P2, SSK, knit to end of the row.
Row 2: Knit the knit stitches and purl the purls.
Repeat rows 1 & 2 7 (8, 9) more times.
When you are done with the decrease instructions, measure the length of the front

piece, comparing it to the back. If the front and back measure the same, bind off the remaining stitches. If the front is too short, continue knitting and purling until the pieces are of equal length, then bind off.

Not Your Standard-Issue Sweatshirt, Take Two
SHAPING THE ARMHOLES:
Note:
Bind off in pattern.
Row 1: Bind off 3 stitches (K1, P1) 4 times, continue in pattern to end of the row.
Row 2: Bind off 3 stitches (P1, K1) 4 times, continue in pattern to end of the row.
Row 3: Bind off 2 stitches (K1, P1) 3 times, continue in pattern to end of the row.
Row 4: Bind off 2 stitches (P1, K1) 3 times, continue in pattern to end of the row.
Row 5: Bind off 1 stitch (P1, K1) 2 times, K1, continue in pattern to end of the row.
Repeat rows 5 & 6 0 (2, 4) more times.

SHAPING THE V-NECK:
Place a marker around the needle in the center of the work.
Row 1: Pattern to 2 stitches before the marker, work 2tog in seed-stitch pattern. This means if the stitch you are about to knit should be a purl, then P2tog; if it should be a knit, then K2tog.
Row 2: Pattern to end. (If you just worked P2tog on the last stitch of the previous row, this row should begin with a purl. If you just worked K2tog, this row should begin with a knit.)
Repeat rows 1 & 2 10 (11, 12) more times.
When you are done with the

decrease instructions, measure the length of the front piece, comparing it to the back. If the front and back measure the same, bind off the remaining stitches. If the front is too short, continue in pattern until the pieces are of equal length, then bind off.

Attach yarn to the other side of the V-neck.
Row 1: Work 2tog in seed-stitch pattern. This means that if the 2nd stitch in should be a purl, then P2tog; if it should be a knit, then K2tog. Pattern to the end of the row.
Row 2: Pattern to the end of the row.
Repeat rows 1 & 2 10 (11, 12) more times.
When you are done with the decrease instructions, measure the length of the front piece, comparing it to the back. If the front and back measure the same, bind off the remaining stitches. If the front is too short, continue in pattern until the pieces are of equal length, then bind off.

CARDIGANS

Give It a Whirl

SHAPING THE ARMHOLES:

BACK:

Row 1: Bind off 4 stitches. Knit to end of the row.
Row 2: Bind off 4 stitches. Purl to end of the row.
Row 3: Bind off 2 stitches. Knit to end of the row.
Row 4: Bind off 2 stitches. Purl to end of the row.
Row 5: K2, SSK, knit to last 4 stitches, K2tog, K2.
Row 6: Purl.
Repeat rows 5 & 6 0 (1, 3) more times.

LEFT FRONT (left side when worn):

You will be binding off on a RS row.
Row 1: Bind off 4 stitches. Knit to end of the row.
Rows 2, 4 & 6: Purl.
Row 3: Bind off 2 stitches. Knit to end of the row.
Row 5: K2, SSK, knit to end of row.
Repeat rows 5 & 6 0 (1, 3) more times.

RIGHT FRONT (right side when worn)

You will be binding off on a WS row.
Row 1: Bind off 4 stitches. Purl to end of the row.
Row 2: Knit.
Row 3: Bind off 2 stitches. Purl to end of the row.
Row 4: Knit to last 4 stitches, K2tog, K2.
Row 5: Purl.
Repeat rows 4 & 5 0 (1, 3) more times.

SHAPING THE V-NECK:

LEFT FRONT (left side when worn):

Row 1: Knit to last 4 stitches, K2tog, K2.
Rows 2 & 4: Purl.
Row 3: Knit.
Repeat rows 1 through 4 8 (9, 9) more times.

RIGHT FRONT (right side when worn):

Row 1: K2, SSK, Knit to end of row.
Rows 2 & 4: Purl.
Row 3: Knit.
Repeat rows 1 through 4 8 (9, 9) more times.
When you are done with the decrease instructions, measure the length of the front piece, comparing it to the back. If the front and back measure the same, bind off the remaining stitches. If the front is too short, continue

knitting and purling until the pieces are of equal length, then bind off.

Fabulously Funky

SHAPING THE A-LINE:

BACK:

Row 1: K2, SSK, knit until 4 stitches remain, K2tog, K2.
Rows 2, 4, 6 & 8: Purl.
Rows 3, 5 & 7: Knit.
Repeat rows 1 through 8 8 (9, 9) more times.

SHAPING THE ARMHOLES:

BACK:

Row 1: Bind off 3 stitches. Knit to end of the row.
Row 2: Bind off 3 stitches. Purl to end of the row.
Row 3: K2, SSK, knit to last 4 stitches, K2tog, K2.
Row 4: Purl.
Repeat rows 3 & 4 1 (2, 2) more time.

LEFT FRONT (left side when worn):

You will be binding off on a RS row.
Row 1: Bind off 3 stitches. Knit to end of the row.
Rows 2 & 4: Purl.
Row 3: K2, SSK, knit to the end of the row.
Repeat rows 3 & 4 1 (2, 2) more time.

RIGHT FRONT (right side when worn):

You will be binding off on a WS row.
Row 1: Bind off 3 stitches. Purl to end of the row.
Row 2: Knit to last 4 stitches, K2tog, K2.
Row 3: Purl.
Repeat rows 2 & 3 1 (2, 2) more time.

SHAPING THE A-LINE:

LEFT FRONT (left side when worn):

Row 1: K2, SSK, knit to end of the row.
Rows 2, 4, 6 & 8: Purl.
Rows 3, 5 & 7: Knit.
Repeat rows 1 through 8 8 (9, 9) more times.

RIGHT FRONT (right side when worn):

Row 1: Knit until 4 stitches remain, K2tog, K2.
Rows 2, 4, 6 & 8: Purl.
Rows 3, 5 & 7: Knit.
Repeat rows 1 through 8 8 (9, 9) more times.

SHAPING THE CREW NECK:

LEFT FRONT (left side when worn):

You will be binding off on a WS row.
Row 1: Bind off 3 stitches. Purl to end of the row.
Rows 2, 4 & 6: Knit.
Row 3: Bind off 2 stitches. Purl to end of the row.
Row 5: Bind off 1 stitch. Purl to end of the row.
Repeat rows 5 & 6 1 (1, 2) more time.
When you are done with the bind-off instructions, measure the length of the front piece, comparing it to the length of the back. If the front and back measure the same, bind off the remaining stitches. If the front is too short, continue in pattern until pieces are of equal length, then bind off.

RIGHT FRONT (right side when worn):

You will be binding off on a RS row.
Row 1: Bind off 3 stitches. Knit to end of the row.
Rows 2, 4 & 6: Purl.
Row 3: Bind off 2 stitches. Knit to end of the row.

Row 5: Bind off 1 stitch. Knit to end of the row.
Repeat rows 5 & 6 1 (1, 2) more time.
When you are done with the bind-off instructions, measure the length of the front piece, comparing it to the length of the back. If the front and back measure the same, bind off the remaining stitches. If the front is too short, continue in pattern until pieces are of equal length, then bind off.

One Singular Sensation

You will not be working the single-stripe method for the armhole and neck shaping. You will need to cut the yarn and attach it where needed.

SHAPING THE ARMHOLES:

BACK:

For Medium & Large:
Row 1: Bind off 4 stitches. Knit to end of the row.
Row 2: Bind off 4 stitches. Purl to end of the row.
For all sizes:
Row 3: Bind off 3 stitches. Knit to end of the row.
Row 4: Bind off 3 stitches. Purl to end of the row.
Row 5: Bind off 2 stitches. Knit to end of the row.
Row 6: Bind off 2 stitches. Purl to end of the row.
Row 7: K2, SSK, knit to last 4 stitches, K2tog, K2.
Row 8: Purl.
Repeat rows 7 & 8 2 (0, 2) more times.

LEFT FRONT (left side when worn):

You will be binding off on a RS row.
For Medium & Large:
Row 1: Bind off 4 stitches. Knit to end of the row.
Row 2: Purl.
For all sizes:
Row 3: Bind off 3 stitches.

Knit to end of the row.
Row 4: Purl.
Row 5: Bind off 2 stitches. Knit to end of the row.
Row 6: Purl.
Row 7: K2, SSK. Knit to end of the row.
Row 8: Purl.
Repeat rows 5 & 6
2 (0, 2) more times.

RIGHT FRONT (right side when worn):

You will be binding off on a WS row.
For Medium & Large:
Row 1: Bind off 4 stitches. Purl to end of the row.
Row 2: Knit.
For all sizes:
Row 3: Bind off 3 stitches. Purl to end of the row.
Row 4: Knit.
Row 5: Bind off 2 stitches. Purl to end of the row.
Row 6: Knit to last 4 stitches, K2tog, K2.
Row 7: Purl.
Repeat rows 4 & 5
2 (0, 2) more times.

SHAPING THE CREW NECK:

LEFT FRONT (left side when worn):

You will be binding off on a WS row.
Row 1: Bind off 5 stitches. Purl to end of the row.
Rows 2, 4, 6 & 8: Knit.
Row 3: Bind off 3 stitches. Purl to end of the row.
Row 5: Bind off 2 stitches. Purl to end of the row.
Row 7: Bind off 1 stitch. Purl to end of the row.
Repeat rows 7 & 8
1 (2, 3) more time.
When you are done with the bind-off instructions, measure the length of the front piece, comparing it to the length of the back. If the front and the back measure the same, bind off the remaining stitches. If the front is too short, continue in pattern

until pieces are of equal length, then bind off.

RIGHT FRONT (right side when worn):

You will be binding off on a RS row.
Row 1: Bind off 5 stitches. Knit to end of the row.
Rows 2, 4, 6 & 8: Purl.
Row 3: Bind off 3 stitches. Knit to end of the row.
Row 5: Bind off 2 stitches. Knit to end of the row.
Row 7: Bind off 1 stitch. Knit to end of the row.
Repeat rows 7 & 8
1 (2, 3) more time.
When you are done with the bind-off instructions, measure the length of the front piece, comparing it to the length of the back. If the front and back measure the same, bind off the remaining stitches. If the front is too short, continue in pattern until pieces are of equal length, then bind off.

Slip and Slide

SHAPING THE ARMHOLES:

BACK:

For Medium & Large:
Row 1: Bind off 3 stitches. Pattern to end of the row.
Row 2: Bind off 3 stitches. Purl to end of the row.
For all sizes:
Row 3: Bind off 2 stitches. Pattern to end of the row.
Row 4: Bind off 2 stitches. Purl to end of the row.
Row 5: K2, SSK, pattern to last 4 stitches, K2tog, K2.
Row 6: Purl.
Repeat rows 5 & 6 2 (0, 1) more times.

LEFT FRONT (left side when worn):

You will be binding off on a RS row.
For Medium & Large:
Row 1: Bind off 3 stitches.

Pattern to end of the row.
Row 2: Purl.
For all sizes:
Row 3: Bind off 2 stitches. Pattern to end of the row.
Row 4: Purl.
Row 5: K2, SSK, pattern to end of the row.
Row 6: Purl.
Repeat rows 5 & 6
2 (0, 1) more times.

RIGHT FRONT (right side when worn):

You will be binding off on a WS row.
For Medium & Large:
Row 1: Bind off 3 stitches. Purl to end of the row.
Row 2: Pattern.
For all sizes:
Row 3: Bind off 2 stitches. Purl to end of the row.
Row 4: Pattern to last 4 stitches, K2tog, K2.
Row 5: Purl.
Repeat rows 4 & 5
2 (0, 1) more times.

SHAPING THE CREW NECK:

LEFT FRONT (left side when worn):

You will be binding off on a WS row.
Row 1: Bind off 3 stitches. Purl to end of the row.
Row 2: Pattern.
Row 3: Bind off 2 stitches. Purl to end of the row.
Row 4: Pattern.
Row 5: Bind off 1 stitch. Purl to end of the row.
Row 6: Pattern.
Repeat rows 5 & 6 0 (1, 1) more times.
When you are done with the bind-off instructions, measure the length of the front piece, comparing it to the length of the back. If the front and back measure the same, bind off the remaining stitches. If the front is too short, continue in pattern until pieces are of equal length, then bind off.

RIGHT FRONT (right side when worn):

You will be binding off on a RS row.

Row 1: Bind off 3 stitches. Pattern to end of the row.

Rows 2, 4 & 6: Purl.

Row 3: Bind off 2 stitches. Pattern to end of the row.

Row 5: Bind off 1 stitch. Pattern to end of the row. Repeat rows 5 & 6 0 (1, 1) more times.

When you are done with the bind-off instructions, measure the length of the front piece, comparing it to the length of the back. If the front and back measure the same, bind off the remaining stitches. If the front is too short, continue in pattern until pieces are of equal length, then bind off.

TEES AND TANKS

A Table for Two

SHAPING THE ARMHOLES:

For Large:

Row 1: Bind off 4 stitches. Knit to end of the row.

Row 2: Bind off 4 stitches. Purl to end of the row.

For all sizes:

Row 3: Bind off 3 stitches. Knit to end of the row.

Row 4: Bind off 3 stitches. Purl to end of the row.

Row 5: Bind off 2 stitches. Knit to end of the row.

Row 6: Bind off 2 stitches. Purl to end of the row.

Row 7: K2, SSK, knit to last 4 stitches, K2tog, K2.

Row 8: Purl.

Repeat rows 7 & 8 0 (3, 2) more times.

SHAPING THE NECK:

Remember that after binding off the center stitches, you will work 1 side at a time.

Row 1: Knit 21 (21, 22) stitches; with the 20th (20th, 21st) stitch begin to bind off the center 14 (16, 16) stitches. For example, for the small size this means you should pull the 20th stitch over the 21st stitch, and this is your first bind-off. When you are done binding off the center 14 (16, 16) stitches, check to make sure you have 19 (19, 20) stitches on each side of the hole, including the stitch on the right needle. Knit to end of row. Turn work.

Rows 2, 4, 6 & 8: Purl.

Row 3: Bind off 3 stitches. Knit to end of the row.

Row 5: Bind off 2 stitches. Knit to end of the row.

Row 7: Bind off 1 stitch. Knit to end of the row.

When you are done with the bind-off instructions, measure the length of the front piece, comparing it to the length of the back. If the front and back measure the same, bind off the remaining stitches. If the front is too short, continue knitting and purling until the pieces are of equal length, then bind off.

For the other side of the neck edge, attach yarn to the remaining stitches at the center of the work (not at the side edge) and begin binding off stitches immediately. You will now be binding off with a WS row facing you. Finish neck shaping as on other side, but purling to the end of the row and knitting the even-numbered rows. Bind off remaining stitches.

The Mysterious Case of the Missing Tee

SHAPING THE ARMHOLES:

For Large:

Row 1: Bind off 4 stitches. Knit to end of the row.

Row 2: Bind off 4 stitches. Purl to end of the row.

For all sizes:

Row 3: Bind off 3 stitches. Knit to end of the row.

Row 4: Bind off 3 stitches. Purl to end of the row.

Row 5: Bind off 2 stitches. Knit to end of the row.

Row 6: Bind off 2 stitches. Purl to end of the row.

Row 7: K2, SSK, knit to last 4 stitches, K2tog, K2.

Row 8: Purl.

Repeat rows 7 & 8 3 (5, 5) more times.

SHAPING THE NECK:

Remember that after binding off the center stitches, you will work 1 side at a time.

Row 1: Pattern 17 (18, 19) stitches; with the 16th (17th, 18th) stitch begin to bind off the center 32 (36, 36) stitches. For example, for the small size, this means you should pull the 16th stitch over the 17th stitch, and this is your first bind-off. When you are done binding off the center 32 (36, 36) stitches, check to make sure you have 15 (16, 17) stitches on each side of the hole, including the stitch on the right needle. Knit to end of row. Turn work.

Row 2: Purl.

Row 3: Knit.

Repeat rows 2 & 3 until piece measures same as the back and bind off.

When you are done with the bind-off instructions, continue in stripe pattern until the pieces are of equal length, then bind off.

For the other side of the neck edge, attach yarn to the remaining stitches at the center of the work. Continue working in stripe pattern until piece measures the same as the back. Bind off all stitches loosely.

A Sweater for the Ages

SHAPING THE ARMHOLES:

For Large:

Row 1: Bind off 4 stitches. Knit to end of the row.

Row 2: Bind off 4 stitches. Purl to end of the row.

For all sizes:

Row 3: Bind off 3 stitches. Knit to end of the row.

Row 4: Bind off 3 stitches. Purl to end of the row.

Row 5: Bind off 2 stitches. Knit to end of the row.

Row 6: Bind off 2 stitches. Purl to end of the row.

Row 7: K2, SSK, knit to last 4 stitches, K2tog, K2.

Row 8: Purl.

Repeat rows 7 & 8 2 (2, 1) more times.

BINDING OFF CENTER STITCHES:

Remember that after binding off the 4 center stitches, you will work 1 side at a time.

Row 1: Pattern 26 (29, 30) stitches; with the 25th (28th, 29th) stitch begin to bind off the center 4 stitches. For example, for the small size, this means you should pull the 25th stitch over the 26th stitch, and this is your first bind-off. When you are done binding off the center 4 stitches, check to make sure you have 24 (27, 28) stitches on each side of the hole, including the stitch on the right needle. Knit to end of row. Turn work.

Row 2: Purl.

Row 3: Knit.

Repeat rows 2 & 3 until piece measures 16.5″ (18″, 19.5″).

SHAPING THE NECK:

RIGHT FRONT (right side when worn):

You will be binding off on a RS row.
Row 1: Bind off 4 stitches. Knit to end of the row.
Row 2: Purl.
Row 3: Bind off 3 stitches. Knit to end of the row.
Rows 4, 6 & 8: Purl.
Row 5: Bind off 2 stitches. Knit to end of the row.
Row 7: Bind off 1 stitch. Knit to end of the row.
Repeat rows 7 & 8
2 (2, 3) more times.
When you are done with the bind-off instructions, measure the length of the front piece, comparing it to the length of the back. If the front and back measure the same, bind off the remaining stitches. If the front is too short, continue in pattern until pieces are of equal length, then bind off.

LEFT FRONT (left side when worn):

Attach yarn to the remaining stitches at the center of the work (not at the side edge) and work in St st until piece measures 16.5″ (18″, 19.5″), ending with a RS row. Then shape neck as follows: You will now be binding off with a WS row facing you. Finish neck shaping as on other side, but purling to the end of the row and knitting the even-numbered row.
Row 1: Bind off 4 stitches. Purl to end of the row.
Row 2: Knit.
Row 3: Bind off 3 stitches. Purl to end of the row.
Rows 4, 6 & 8: Knit.
Row 5: Bind off 2 stitches. Purl to end of the row.

Row 7: Bind off 1 stitch. Purl to end of the row.
Repeat rows 7 & 8
2 (2, 3) more times.
When you are done with the bind-off instructions, measure the length of the front piece, comparing it to the length of the back. If the front and back measure the same, bind off the remaining stitches. If the front is too short, continue in pattern until pieces are of equal length, then bind off.

Tank You Very Much

SHAPING THE ARMHOLES:

Row 1: Bind off 4 stitches. Knit to end of the row.
Row 2: Bind off 4 stitches. Purl to end of the row.
Row 3: Bind off 3 stitches. Knit to end of the row.
Row 4: Bind off 3 stitches. Purl to end of the row.
Row 5: Bind off 2 stitches. Knit to end of the row.
Row 6: Bind off 2 stitches. Purl to end of the row.
Row 7: K2, SSK, knit to last 4 stitches, K2tog, K2.
Row 8: Purl.
Repeat rows 7 & 8
0 (2, 5) more times.

SHAPING THE NECK:

Remember that after binding off the center stitches, you will work 1 side at a time.
Row 1: Pattern 22 (24, 25) stitches; with the 21st (23rd, 24th) stitch begin to bind off the center 20 (22, 24) stitches. For example, for the small size, this means you should pull the 21st stitch over the 22nd stitch, and this is your first bind-off. When you are done binding off the center 20 (22, 24) stitches, check to make sure you have 20 (22, 23) stitches on each side of the hole, including the stitch on the right needle. Knit to

end of the row. Turn work.
Rows 2, 4, 6, 8 & 10: Purl.
Row 3: Bind off 3 stitches. Knit to end of the row.
Row 5: Bind off 2 stitches. Knit to end of the row.
Row 7: Bind off 1 stitch. Knit to end of the row.
Row 9: Bind off 1 stitch. Knit to end of the row.
When you are done with the bind-off instructions, measure the length of the front piece, comparing it to the length of the back. If the front and back measure the same, bind off the remaining stitches. If the front is too short, continue knitting and purling until the pieces are of equal length, then bind off.

For the other side of the neck edge, attach yarn to the remaining stitches at the center of the work (not at the side edge) and begin binding off stitches immediately. You will now be binding off with a WS row facing you. Finish neck shaping as on other side, but purling to the end of the row and knitting the even-numbered rows.

The Same . . . but Different

SHAPING THE ARMHOLES:

For Large:
Row 1: Bind off 4 stitches. Knit to end of the row.
Row 2: Bind off 4 stitches. Purl to end of the row.
For all sizes:
Row 3: Bind off 3 stitches. Knit to end of the row.
Row 4: Bind off 3 stitches. Purl to end of the row.
Row 5: Bind off 2 stitches. Knit to end of the row.
Row 6: Bind off 2 stitches. Purl to end of the row.
Row 7: K2, SSK, knit to last 4 stitches, K2tog, K2.
Row 8: Purl.

Repeat rows 7 & 8 3 (5, 4) more times.

SHAPING THE NECK:

Remember that after binding off the center stitches, you will work 1 side at a time.
Row 1: Pattern 23 (25, 26) stitches; with the 22nd (24th, 25th) stitch begin to bind off the center 18 (20, 22) stitches. For example, for the small size, this means you should pull the 22nd stitch over the 23rd stitch, and this is your first bind-off. When you are done binding off the center 18 (20, 22) stitches, check to make sure you have 21 (23, 24) stitches on each side of the hole, including the stitch on the right needle. Knit to end of row. Turn work.
Row 2: Purl.
Row 3: Bind off 3 stitches. Knit to end of the row.
Row 4: Purl.
Row 5: Bind off 2 stitches. Knit to end of the row.
Row 6: Purl.
Row 7: Bind off 1 stitch. Knit to end of the row.
Row 8: Purl.
Repeat rows 7 & 8 twice more.
When you are done with the bind-off instructions, measure the length of the front piece, comparing it to the length of the back. If the front and back measure the same, bind off the remaining stitches. If the front is too short, continue knitting and purling until the pieces are of equal length, then bind off.

For the other side of the neck edge, attach yarn to the remaining stitches at the center of the work (not at the side edge) and begin binding off stitches immediately. You will now be binding off with a WS row facing you. Finish neck shaping as on other side, but purling to the end of the row and knitting the even-numbered rows.

Tara's Tank

SHAPING THE ARMHOLES:

Row 1: Bind off 3 stitches. Knit to end of the row.
Row 2: Bind off 3 stitches. Purl to end of the row.
Row 3: Bind off 2 stitches. Knit to end of the row.
Row 4: Bind off 2 stitches. Purl to end of the row.
Row 5: K2, SSK, knit to last 4 stitches, K2tog, K2.
Row 6: Purl.
Repeat rows 7 & 8 0 (1, 1) more times.

SHAPING THE V-NECK:

Place a marker around the needle in the center of the work.
Row 1: Knit until 9 stitches before the marker, K2tog, P4, K3.
Row 2: P3, K4, purl to end of the row.
Repeat rows 1 & 2 9 (10, 11) more times.
When you are done with the decrease instructions, measure the length of the front piece, comparing it to the back. If the front and back measure the same, bind off the remaining stitches. If the front is too short, continue working in pattern until the pieces are of equal length, then bind off.

Attach yarn to the other side of the V-neck.
Row 1: K3, P4, SSK, knit to end of the row.
Row 2: Purl until 7 stitches remain, K4, P3.
Repeat rows 1 & 2 9 (10, 11) more times.
When you are done with the decrease instructions, measure the length of the front piece, comparing it to the back. If the front and back measure the same, bind off the remaining stitches. If the front is too short, continue working in pattern until the pieces are of equal length, then bind off.

Hip and Hooded

BINDING OFF CENTER STITCHES:

Remember that after binding off the 6 center stitches, you will work 1 side at a time. Continue working in St st with the decreases on the outside edges until piece measures 21.5″ (23.5″, 25.5″) from cast-on edge.

SHAPING THE NECK:

RIGHT FRONT (right side when worn):
You will be binding off on the RS row.
Row 1: Bind off 3 stitches. Knit to end of the row.
Row 2: Purl.
Row 3: Bind off 3 stitches. Knit to end of the row.
Row 4: Purl.
Row 5: Bind off 2 stitches. Knit to end of the row.
Row 6: Purl.
Row 7: Bind off 1 stitch. Knit to end of the row.
Row 8: Purl.

Repeat rows 7 & 8 0 (1, 1) more times.
Bind off remaining stitch.
For the other side of the neck edge, attach yarn to the remaining stitches at the center of the work (not at the side edge) and begin binding off stitches immediately. You will now be binding off with a WS row facing you. Finish neck shaping as on other side, but purling to the end of the row and knitting the even-numbered rows. Bind off remaining stitch.

INDEX

ABOUT THE AUTHORS

Inveterate knitters since college, Jordana Jacobs and Julie Carles left their respective careers in the medical and legal worlds to assume ownership of the Yarn Company, New York City's landmark knitting store since 1997. The store has become a destination for celebrities and locals alike, who come in for the quickly sold-out classes, unrivaled yarn selection, customized knitting patterns—and friendly conversation. The Yarn Company can be reached on the web at www.theyarnco.com. Julie and Jordana live in New York City. They are the authors of *The Yarn Girls' Guide to Simple Knits* and *The Yarn Girls' Guide to Kid Knits*.

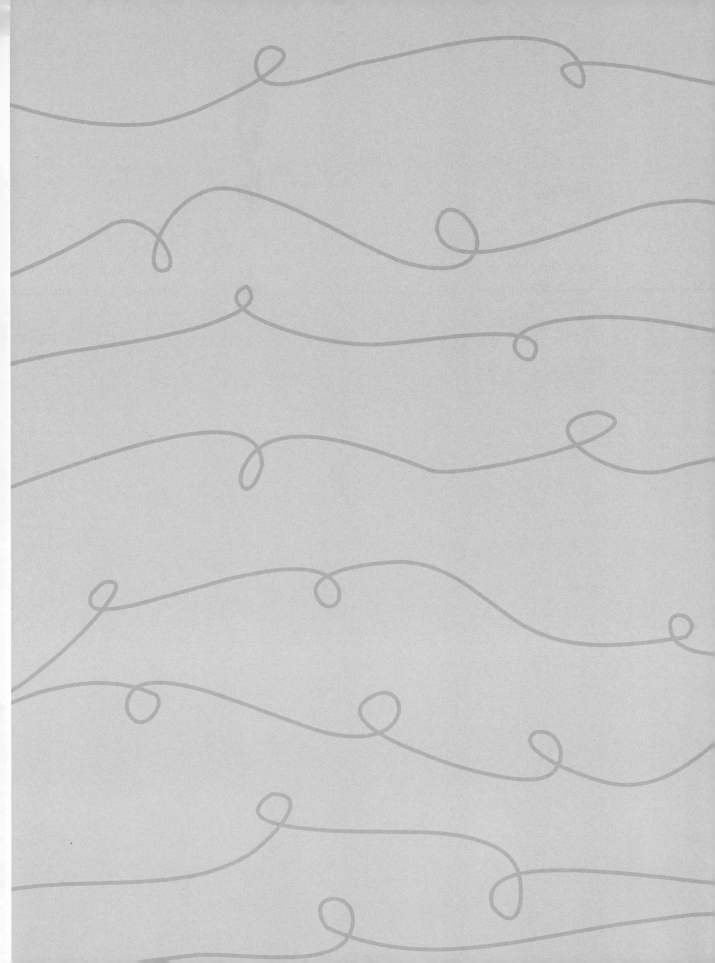